CENTRIC 2016

The Ninth International Conference on Advances in Human oriented and Personalized Mechanisms, Technologies, and Services

August 21 - 25, 2016

Rome, Italy

CENTRIC 2016 Editors

Lasse Berntzen, Vestfold University College - Tønsberg, Norway

Stephan Böhm, RheinMain University of Applied Sciences - Wiesbaden, Germany

Printed from e-media with permission by:

Curran Associates, Inc.
57 Morehouse Lane
Red Hook, NY 12571

Some format issues inherent in the e-media version may also appear in this print version.

Printed by Curran Associates, Inc. (2016)

International Academy, Research, and Industry Association (IARIA)
412 Derby Way
Wilmington, DE 19810

Phone: (408) 893-6407
Fax: (408) 527-6351

petre@iaria.org

Additional copies of this publication are available from:

Curran Associates, Inc.
57 Morehouse Lane
Red Hook, NY 12571 USA
Phone: 845-758-0400
Fax: 845-758-2633
Email: curran@proceedings.com
Web: www.proceedings.com

TABLE OF CONTENTS

CENTRIL 1: USER-CENTRIC SYSTEMS

CENTRIC 2: PRIVACY AND APPLICATIONS

CENTRIC 3 / POSETE: POLLUTANTS SENSING TECHNIQUES FOR HUMAN HEALTH DAMAGES ESTIMATION

CENTRIC 2016

Forward

The Ninth International Conference on Advances in Human-oriented and Personalized Mechanisms, Technologies, and Services (CENTRIC 2016), held on August 21 - 25, 2016 in Rome, Italy, addressed topics on human-oriented and personalized mechanisms, technologies, and services, commonly known as I-centric.

There is a cohort of technologies that favored the so called "user-centric" services and applications. While some of them reached some maturity, others are to prove their economics (WiMax, IPTV, RFID, etc). The human-oriented and personalized technologies and services rely on a key set of features, some to be deployed, others getting more mature (personal profiles, preferences, identity, proximity, personal devices, etc.). Following, advanced applications covering human related activities benefit from personalized and human-oriented networks and services, especially preventive and personalized medicine, body networks and devices, or anticipative systems.

The conference provided a forum where researchers were able to present recent research results and new research problems and directions related to them. The conference sought contributions presenting novel result and future research in all aspects of user-centric mechanisms, technologies, and services.

Similar to the previous editions, this event continued to be very competitive in its selection process and very well perceived by the international community. As such, it attracted excellent contributions and active participation from all over the world. We were very pleased to receive a large amount of top quality contributions.

We take here the opportunity to warmly thank all the members of the CENTRIC 2016 technical program committee as well as the numerous reviewers. The creation of such a broad and high quality conference program would not have been possible without their involvement. We also kindly thank all the authors that dedicated much of their time and efforts to contribute to the CENTRIC 2016. We truly believe that thanks to all these efforts, the final conference program consists of top quality contributions.

This event could also not have been a reality without the support of many individuals, organizations and sponsors. We also gratefully thank the members of the CENTRIC 2016 organizing committee for their help in handling the logistics and for their work that is making this professional meeting a success.

We hope the CENTRIC 2016 was a successful international forum for the exchange of ideas and results between academia and industry and to promote further progress in personalization research. We also hope Rome provided a pleasant environment during the conference and everyone saved some time for exploring this beautiful historic city.

CENTRIC 2016 General Chairs

Lasse Berntzen, University College of Southeast, Norway
Stephan Böhm, RheinMain University of Applied Sciences - Wiesbaden, Germany

CENTRIC Advisory Committee

Michael Gebhart, iteratec GmbH, Germany
Vitaly Klyuev, University of Aizu, Japan
Mario Hoffmann, Fraunhofer-Institute for Secure Information Technology (SIT) - Darmstadt, Germany
Guadalupe Ortiz, University of Cádiz, Spain
Thomas Marx, University of Applied Sciences Bingen, Germany
Inmaculada Rodriguez Santiago, University of Barcelona, Spain

CENTRIC 2016 Research Institute Liaison Chairs

R. Hariprakash, Arulmighu Meenakashi Amman College of Engineering, India
Muhammad Iftikhar, International Medical School - Management & Science University (MSU), Malaysia

CENTRIC 2016 Industry/Research Chairs

Rainer Falk, Siemens AG - München, Deutschland

CENTRIC 2016

Committee

CENTRIC 2016 General Chairs

Lasse Berntzen, University College of Southeast, Norway
Stephan Böhm, RheinMain University of Applied Sciences - Wiesbaden, Germany

CENTRIC Advisory Committee

Michael Gebhart, iteratec GmbH, Germany
Vitaly Klyuev, University of Aizu, Japan
Mario Hoffmann, Fraunhofer-Institute for Secure Information Technology (SIT) - Darmstadt, Germany
Guadalupe Ortiz, University of Cádiz, Spain
Thomas Marx, University of Applied Sciences Bingen, Germany
Inmaculada Rodriguez Santiago, University of Barcelona, Spain

CENTRIC 2016 Research Institute Liaison Chairs

R. Hariprakash, Arulmighu Meenakashi Amman College of Engineering, India
Muhammad Iftikhar, International Medical School - Management & Science University (MSU), Malaysia

CENTRIC 2016 Industry/Research Chairs

Rainer Falk, Siemens AG - München, Deutschland

CENTRIC 2016 Technical Program Committee

Mohammed A. Akour, Yarmouk University, Jordan
Ana Almeida, Institute of Engineering - Polytechnic of Porto, Portugal
Giner Alor Hernandez, Instituto Tecnologico de Orizaba, México
Rémi Bastide, Université Champollion, France
Carlos Becker Westphall, Federal University of Santa Catarina, Brazil
Stephan Böhm, RheinMain University, Germany
Mahmoud Boufaida, Mentouri University of Constantine, Algeria
Mahmoud Brahimi, University of Msila, Algeria
Lillian Brandão, Universidade Federal de Minas Gerais (UFMG), Brazil
Gerd Bruder, University of Hamburg, Germany
Marco Bruti, Telecom Italia Sparkle S.p.A. - Roma, Italy
Daniel Bo-Wei Chen, School of Information Technology - Monash University Sunway Campus, Malaysia
Umberto Cerasani, Sophia Antipolis, France
Feng Cheng, Hasso-Plattner-Institute at University of Potsdam, Germany
Sabine Coquillart, INRIA, France
Carlos J. Costa, ISCTE-IUL, Portugal

Ignazio Passero, University of Salerno, Italy
Cathryn Peoples, Queen Mary University of London, UK
Isabel Pereira Marcelino, Polytechnic Institute of Leiria, Portugal
Willy Picard, Poznan University of Economics, Poland
Anna Puig, University of Barcelona, Spain
Valentim Realinho, Polytechnic Institute of Portalegre, Portugal
Ann Reddipogu, ManyWorlds UK Ltd. - Aberdeen, UK
Karen Renaud, University of Glasgow, UK
Michele Risi, University of Salerno, Italy
Joel Rodrigues, University of Beira Interior, Portugal
Marcos Rodrigues, Sheffield Hallam University, UK
Inmaculada Rodriguez Santiago, University of Barcelona, Spain
Carmen Santero, CNR-ISTI, Italy
Marcello Sarini, Università degli Studi Milano-Bicocca - Milano, Italy
Nilanjan Sarkar, Vanderbilt University, USA
Narasimha K. Shashidhar, Sam Houston State University, USA
Dominique L. Scapin INRIA, France
Guillaume Schaff, itrust consulting, Luxembourg
Peter Schartner, Universität Klagenfurt, Austria
Friedhelm Schwenker, University of Ulm, Germany
Monica M. L. Sebillo, University of Salerno, Italy
Jacques Simonin, Institut Télécom / Télécom Bretagne, France
Luciano P. Soares, Insper, Brazil
Christophe Strobbe, Stuttgart Media University, Germany
Mu-Chun Su, National Central University, Taiwan
Weilian Su, Naval Postgraduate School - Monterey, USA
Roman Y. Shtykh, CyberAgent, Inc., Japan
Hung-Min Sun, National Tsing Hua University, Taiwan
Ruck Thawonmas, Ritsumeikan University, Japan
Genoveffa Tortora, University of Salerno, Italy
Jacques Traoré, Orange Labs, France
Carlos Travieso González, University of Las Palmas de Gran Canaria, Spain
Giuliana Vitiello, Università degli studi di Salerno, Italy
Robin Vivian, Université de Lorraine, France
Evangelos Vlachogiannis, Fraunhofer Institute for Applied Information Technology FIT, Germany
Florian Volk, Technische Universität Darmstadt, Germany
Konstantinos Votis, Information Technologies Institute, Greece
Nan Wang, Linkedin.com, USA
Benjamin Weyers, University of Duisburg-Essen, Germany
Sherali Zeadally, University of Kentucky, USA
Haifeng (Kevin) Zhao, University of California - Davis, USA

Copyright Information

Mobile Recruiting Beyond Job Search: A User-Centered Approach for Smartphone-Based Job Applications

Stephan Böhm
RheinMain University of Applied Sciences
Department of Media Management
Wiesbaden, Germany
e-mail: stephan.boehm@hs-rm.de

Wolfgang Achilles
Jobware Online
Service GmbH
Paderborn, Germany
e-mail: w.achilles@jobware.de

Abstract—**This paper presents a user-centered approach to identify user requirements for smartphone-based job applications. Initial user requirements were derived from a questionnaire within a smartphone-affine user group. The survey findings were then used to generate low- and high-fidelity prototypes of a mobile app supporting job applications. The prototypes were tested to collect user feedback and to improve their functionality and usability. As a result, some key recommendations for the implementation of smartphone-supported job application processes can be presented at the end of this paper.**

Keywords-Mobile recruiting; mobile job applications; user-centered design; mobile application; mobile usage behavior.

I. INTRODUCTION

According to the GSM Association, worldwide mobile Internet penetration reached 44 percent at the end of 2015 and is predicted to grow to 60 percent of the world population by the end of the decade in 2020. In the same time period, mobile Internet penetration is expected to increase from 66 percent to 77 percent in the developed countries [1]. The growth of mobile Internet changes user behavior and shifts information retrieval activities from desktop to mobile devices. In mid-2015, Google searches on mobile devices already exceeded those on computers in ten countries including the US and Japan [2]. Drivers of the development are a greater availability and affordability of smartphones as well as broadband mobile network infrastructures. Smartphone adoption rate in the developed world was already 65 percent of the connection base at the end of 2015 [1].

Smartphones connected to the mobile Internet can be used to access a wide variety of information for very different purposes. One field of application is the search for job-related information by job seekers. Access to this kind of information via smartphone depends on how the content and its presentation is adapted to the special requirements and limitations of mobile devices. Despite the considerable technical improvements achieved, mobile devices are still characterized by smaller displays, limited keyboards, as well as less processing power and memory compared to desktop computers. For this reason, the web-based offerings of job-related information like career websites and job portals need to be optimized for access by mobile devices to provide an adequate user or "candidate" experience. Another reason why this is business critical for employers is that search engines like Google have started to consider mobile-friendliness of websites as a ranking factor [3]. Mobile-friendly web pages will appear higher on search results which corresponds with a higher chance to be recognized and clicked by mobile job seekers.

Responsive web design is one popular technical approach to provide an improved user experience of websites across multiple devices [4]. Besides this, the structure and the content needs to be adapted to the requirements of a mobile usage context (e.g., text adapted to shorter attention span). Another approach to provide a mobile-optimized candidate experience is to provide job-related information via mobile applications. Besides the device limitations mentioned above, the use of mobile technology can enable organizations to find new ways to attract or hire potential candidates. Examples are the use of QR codes in job advertisements to provide additional job-related information or to filter job offers by the jobseekers' current location. The use of innovative mobile technologies for recruiting purposes is often referred to as "mobile recruiting". More precisely, mobile recruiting can be defined as "... any organizational information provided for or delivered to a mobile device in order to attract and hire potential applicants and employees" [5]. It can be interpreted as a field of e-recruiting that deals with the challenges and opportunities of deploying mobile technologies along the whole "recruiting funnel". This recruiting process begins with the use of mobile media to increase awareness of the employer brand and it ends with the support of the candidate's application via mobile devices [6].

In contrast to the mobile recruiting activities for job search, the job application is a more interactive process. For example, candidates might need to submit comprehensive application documents to the prospective employer or want to include a cover letter to highlight particular qualifications for a job. Smartphone user interfaces are not designed for extensive text input or document management efficiently. This is why a mobile-optimization of the job application cannot be confined to the adaptation of the job-related content and its presentation. Rather, the complete application process has to be redefined and aligned for smartphone-based job applications.

Against this background, the aim of this study is to identify user requirements of such a mobile-optimized job application process. Following this introduction, the research background and objectives with regards to mobile job applications are discussed in Section II. The study's user-centered design approach is the subject of Section III before the key findings are presented in Section IV. The paper concludes with best-practice recommendations for the implementation of the mobile application process in Section V and the study's limitations and an outlook on further research in Section VI.

II. RESEARCH BACKGROUND AND OBJECTIVES

According to the results of a global IBM Work Trends Study from 2015, more than half of all job seekers (53 percent) used their mobile devices to search for a job. The most typical mobile job seekers' activities are the search for job postings (74 percent) or job-related information (55 percent) and to get job alerts (54 percent). Less common within the group of mobile job seekers is the use of mobile devices to express job interest (35 percent) or taking job-related assessments (18 percent) [7]. Use of mobile devices for job search also changed job seeker behavior. Job search with mobile devices is a less focused and planned activity than something that occurs incidentally and often done to fill waiting or idle time during the day. According to Jobvite [8], most of the job seekers (32 percent) spend between six and ten minutes on mobile devices for job searches. Common situations for mobile job search mentioned in this study are in bed (47 percent), during commute (38 percent), in a restaurant (36 percent), on the job (30 percent), during a meeting (21 percent) and even in the restroom (18 percent).

While job search via mobile devices is becoming more and more common, applying for a job using a smartphone is still less popular. With regard to the IBM study mentioned before, only 25 percent of the global employees who have used mobile in their job search also completed entire job applications on this device [7]. The user acceptance to apply mobile varies between countries. A recent study carried out by the job portal provider Careerbuilder reports that 9 percent applied for a job on a mobile device in the US but 14 percent in Germany. The main reasons to not apply mobile in both countries (US; Germany) are the lack of a full keyboard (53; 58 percent), too small screens (47; 44 percent), problems regarding the availability of a resume on the device (30; 21 percent), the creation of personalized cover letters (18; 25 percent) or the perception that this way of applying is too hard in general (19; 16 percent) [9][10]. This industry research shows that there is a gap between mobile job searching and application behavior and that there are some usage barriers which need to be overcome.

However, more detailed findings on user expectations and requirements as well as more concrete recommendations on how to design a mobile-optimized job application process are not revealed within these studies. Similarly, empirical knowledge and findings from scientific research on mobile job applications are still rare. Only few authors have identified mobile recruiting as an object for research or considered it to be a trend within e-recruiting during the last five years. The majority of these publications discuss the status quo [5], challenges and opportunities for HR and personnel recruitment [11][12][13][14] as well as factors influencing user acceptance of this new recruiting channel [15][16][17]. Some more industry-oriented publications have analyzed mobile job seeker behavior [6] as well as mobile-optimization [18] or video-enhancement of job advertisements [19]. The authors of this paper are not aware of any article that has analyzed the user requirements for mobile job applications.

Summarizing the discussion above, it can be stated that there is a research deficit and a demand in practice to gain knowledge on the user-oriented design of mobile job application processes. In this regard, this study has the following three objectives:

- *Describe the status quo* of job applications via mobile devices from the employer and the candidate perspective: The focus is on early adopters and the group of young talents in Germany.
- *Identify basic user requirements* with regard to the mobile job application process and deduce some fundamental best-practice recommendations for a user-centric design of such a process.
- *Generate a prototype* for an app-based mobile job application support as a basis for initial user testing and feedback-based improvements.

As this work was conducted in cooperation with a job portal provider, the focus of this study was application-oriented research with the aim to generate scientific knowledge that can be applied in the further development of job portal systems.

III. RESEARCH METHODOLOGY

The previous section revealed that the support of job applications by smartphones is a relatively new topic and can be assumed to a certain extent to be unknown within the target groups of recruiters. In this situation, the identification of user requirements cannot be based solely on user surveys. For this reason, this study is built around a user-centered design approach. User-centered Design (UCD) can be seen as a "... methodology used by developers and designers to ensure they're creating products that meet users' needs" [20]. The basic idea is to involve users at a very early stage of the development to acquire information on users' expectations, behavior, and perceptions in order to continuously evolve and improve the product design in an iterative and interactive process [21]. A key element of UCD are prototypes. Prototypes demonstrate and visualize a design idea prior to implementation, enable user experiments with design variations, as well as clarification of user requirements. They are a communication tool between the different stakeholders in the product design and development process [22]. A UCD process can be structured in five phases: initial assessment, upfront user research, design and development, implementation, and market introduction [21][23]. The focus of this study is on the first three phases and thus the early stages within the UCD process.

- *Initial assessment:* In a first step, the general objectives and requirements need to be defined. The objective is to present a user-centered concept for an app that enables users to apply for jobs by smartphone. As there are already existing solutions to enable mobile job application, we started this study with an in-depth competitive user experience analysis [23]. For this purpose, the recruiting apps and websites of the 30 highest-turnover companies (2014) in Germany as well as 14 websites of job portals and 21 related mobile apps were analyzed. The objective of this initial assessment was to (1) outline the status quo on the implementation status in Germany, (2) identify components and process steps from the employer perspective as well as (3) best-practices and what to avoid with regard to the current implementation status.

- *Up-front user-research:* The results of the initial phase were then structured by using a morphological box approach [24]. The parameters of this box were defined by the identified components and process steps of a generic mobile job application process. Therefore, the employer-driven perspective from the initial assessment was extended and completed by a user journey for a mobile application process derived from expert discussion. As a result, a two-dimensional morphological box was created with process steps and components as a first dimension and a varying number of corresponding implementation variants as a second dimension. Each combination of implementation variants along the process steps and components represents a possible implementation of a mobile application process. The result was then used to identify areas where the knowledge of user preferences could help to reduce the number of implementation variants that need to be considered for prototyping and user testing. For this purpose, a questionnaire was developed and used to collect feedback on user preferences of young talents within the German job-applicant market. The questionnaire was distributed online and offline among media-affine students in Germany by using a convenient sampling method. The survey contained 29 questions on the participants' general job application behavior as well as experiences and expectations towards mobile job applications. The survey was actively distributed from December 7th to 30th, 2015 and resulted in a data sample of 382 participants.
- *Design and development:* The prototypes for user testing were generated in the last step of this study. Scribbles of screen designs were developed for each of the process steps and the user interface components along the generic user journey mentioned above. This was necessary to identify elements within the screen flow that can be separated from each other or need to be combined. The resulting library of user interface patterns was then used to deploy the empirical findings from the questionnaire to define user-oriented job-application process variants as a subject of further user testing. The process variants identified were then discussed with experts for job portals and transferred into first interactive high-fidelity prototypes using the mobile prototyping tool proto.io [25]. Based on two prototype variants, demo videos were produced. This was in order to be able to present a standardized stimulus and to reduce complexity as it was not possible to generate an interactive prototype in this phase that supports all the features required for a realistic screen flow (e.g., cloud upload, text recognition). Each demo video was then presented to test users (18 and 17 participants) between January 20th and 22nd, 2015. Feedback was collected based on a questionnaire at the end of the sessions and used to develop improved prototypes summarizing the study's findings.

To sum up, on the basis of the above, the procedure presented can be categorized as a (sequential) multi-method or mixed-method approach combining qualitative and quantitative approaches. The study is focused on the early stages within a UCD process to generate knowledge about user requirements with regard to a smartphone-supported job-application process. Intended outcomes are a prototype visualizing the mobile-optimized and user-oriented mobile job-application process as well as best-practices or recommendations on how to fulfill user requirements.

IV. STUDY RESULTS

Following the presented approach and for the sake of brevity the presentation of the study's results, in this section, will focus on selected findings: (1) market analysis, (2) user survey and (3) key characteristics of the prototype.

A. *Market Analysis*

Only five of the analyzed career websites of the 30 highest-turnover companies in Germany support a mobile job application. In most cases (4), the applicants have to enter their profile data manually. Some of the employers (2) offer an option to import this data from (business-oriented) social networking services. Application documents can be uploaded from the smartphone (4). One company supports mobile applications and abstains entirely from additional documents. An option to upload from a cloud service was not offered by any website. Only three of the 30 companies offer a mobile app with an option to apply for jobs. Two of these apps support the creation of a candidate profile by text entry or import from social network providers. The findings demonstrate that mobile job applications are not yet of any great importance for German top employers. However, some innovators have started to test the applicability and possibilities of this new recruiting channel and integrated features beyond the traditional online application. Among those features identified in the analysis are video-based applications, options to give feedback on the application process, or include text recognition capabilities that reduce the necessity of extensive text entry.

The situation is slightly different for the job portals. Five of the 14 popular job portal websites investigated provide an option to apply via a mobile device. One without and four with the requirement of user registration. Application documents can be uploaded from the smartphone (4) or –again rarely supported– by cloud services (1). However, support of smartphone-based job applications appears to be a domain of mobile apps from job portals and related service providers. Fifteen of the 21 apps analyzed offered such an option. Candidates can apply in different ways: directly without registration (5), after they have registered at a job portal (10), or by using an existing login from a social network (8). The picture is more mixed regarding the collection of candidate information. Most of the apps (9) required manual text entry for the profile data. Five apps offered an option to apply without resumes and cover letters. The support to submit additional candidate information of the other apps varied in terms of the type of documents between uploads, social network import or manual text entries.

The findings from the market research were consolidated with feedback from job portal experts and summarized in a list of fundamental mobile application components and implementation variants as presented in Table 1.

TABLE I. FUNDAMENTAL MOBILE JOB APPLICATION COMPONENTS AND IMPLEMENTATION VARIANTS

Login/ Registration	No registration, register account, register with existing social network account (e.g., LinkedIn, XING)
Candidate Profile	None, text entry, import from job portal, import from social network profile
Photo	Camera, gallery, cloud upload (e.g., Dropbox), import from social media profile
Cover Letter	None, free text, predefined text templates and blocks, customizable text, text entry structured by questions, upload (non-editable), upload and text recognition (import for editing), video-based self-presentation
Submission	None, text entry, form, local upload, cloud upload
Resume	None, free text, text entry structured by questions, upload (non-editable), upload and text recognition (import for editing)
Submission	None, text entry, form, local upload, cloud upload, import from job portal, import from social network profile
Certificates	None, grades only, free text, scanned documents
Submission	None, text entry, form, local upload, cloud upload
User Control	None, confirmations, save and submit later
Guidance	None, status bar, tooltips, popups

These results of the market analysis were then used to define a questionnaire to identify user requirements and preferences with regard to the implementation variants as discussed in Section III.

B. *User Survey*

The questionnaire on the user preferences and requirements was completed by 382 respondents. As mentioned in Section III, the survey was conducted as a convenience sample and thus reflects more or less the demographics of the Media Management students at RheinMain University. The average age of the respondents was 22 years and 64 percent of the participants were female. The majority of the students are studying for a bachelor degree (78 percent) and 54 percent will graduate by 2017.

Almost all the participants own a smartphone (99 percent) with Android being the most used mobile operating system (50 percent). Facebook is the most popular social network and 81 percent use it often or regularly. Business-oriented social networks are only used regularly by a very small proportion of the young talents (LinkedIn: 1 percent; XING: 2 percent). In this regard, it can already be assumed that importing candidate profiles from this type of social network –as is already offered by German career websites and job portals– is not an adequate option for this specific target group. Dropbox is the most common cloud service, regularly or often used by 63 percent of the participants (Google drive: 14 percent; OneDrive: 5 percent).

The majority of the young talents have experience with job applications: 39 percent have applied for a job within the last six months and 14 percent were currently seeking a job. Most of the jobs in scope are internships (30 percent), part-time jobs (24 percent) or working student positions (18 percent). About 70 percent send between one and five applications when seeking a job. Seventy-one percent manage to complete the preparation of a job application within one hour. The perceived importance of candidate information varies by type of document (important or rather important): resume (94 percent), cover letter (83 percent), certificates (77 percent), and photo (46 percent). The most popular platform to search for a job is still the desktop computer. More than half (54 percent) of the respondents stated that they always use a computer. Mobile devices are still less popular for job searches. A smartphone is always (often) used for job search by only 6 percent (22 percent) of the respondents.

The study participants had little or no experience with job applications via mobile devices. Less than one fifth (17 percent) had ever seen such an option and only 7 percent have already applied for a job from a mobile device. However, the low level of experience seems to be more a result of a lack of opportunities than a lack of interest. Half of the respondents are open-minded towards this new way to apply for a job. The majority of those who can imagine applying mobile stated that such an option is a contemporary requirement (79 percent), should be offered more often (61 percent), and can be expected from innovative employers (56 percent). The main reasons to use such an option are non-availability of computer access (79 percent), applying while being on-the-go (68 percent), to make an initial contact (67 percent), or if such an option is less complicated and more convenient to use (66 percent). Only 9 percent would apply via mobile if they could do so by submitting a video-based application.

The main causes of concerns with regard to applying with a smartphone are uncomfortable and awkward text entry (82 percent) as well as small screens (81 percent) and unreliable Internet connections (71 percent). Beside these more technical problems, the respondents are concerned with regard to limited possibilities for self-presentation (46 percent) and the acceptance of mobile job applications by HR departments (45 percent). With regard to the application documents, most of the study participants consider it likely that they would prepare a cover letter on the computer (72 percent) or make only small modifications with the smartphone keyboard (59 percent). Even short text entry was more accepted (37 percent) than relying on standardized text modules (18 percent) or always reusing the same cover letter unchanged (15 percent). The most preferred option for uploading information was a local upload from the smartphone. This might be due to privacy concerns when uploading the documents via the Internet. With this regard it was a surprise that the study participants would rather upload from a cloud service (e.g., Dropbox) than use a job portal provider as a repository for their application documents.

C. Prototype

Prototypes were designed to acquire more knowledge on the submission of candidate information like cover letter, resume, and certificates that revealed to be critical for user acceptance based on the results of the user survey. In addition to a base case scenario, a prototype variant supporting "one-click applications" was designed. The prototypes were subject to user testing and improved based on the user feedback in two successive stages. The most important result from the prototyping phase was the requirement to provide a high level of guidance (e.g., show current and required steps for completion) and control (e.g., details of required documents and submission status). Unexpectedly, and contrary to the survey results, the majority (71 percent) of the participants refused to accept "one-click applications" after being exposed to the corresponding prototype. This might be due to the fact that the effort on the user side was quite similar for both prototype variants. Moreover, the one-click application function required some additional input for the personalization of a re-usable candidate profile. This is why the advantages of the one-click application for the user become apparent only when the candidate reuses the pre-prepared information for multiple applications. It turned out that a demo video to demonstrate the prototype functionality might be insufficient to convey such a user experience.

V. Conclusion

The growing shift of Internet usage from desktop to mobile devices puts increasing pressure on employers to provide a continuous mobile-optimized candidate experience over the entire recruiting process. Likewise applying for a job directly from a smartphone will become more and more common and expected especially by upcoming job seeker generations. Meanwhile, smartphone support can be introduced selectively to benefit from a potential faster response or lower barriers to submitting a job application. This study revealed important user requirements that have to be considered for a successful implementation:

- *Links to profiles in business networks cannot substitute the submission of application documents.* This is because business networks (e.g., XING, LinkedIn) are not very popular in the group of young talents investigated in this study.
- *Upload and cloud functions need to be integrated for document upload.* Candidates prefer public cloud services like Dropbox to a document upload to job portal providers.
- *Extensive text entry needs to be avoided but options for application document individualization are absolutely essential.* Usability can be increased by offering text recognition capabilities (to make documents editable) and pre-structured formats and layouts (e.g., resume).
- *Employers need to actively dispel candidates' reservations to apply via mobile.* Employers should reduce the uncertainty about the employer's acceptance of mobile applications by more actively promoting this new hiring channel.
- *Simplicity is the key.* Employers have to reduce the amount of required candidate information to the minimum necessary or allow "one-click applications" with pre-prepared documents. Again, the acceptance of such "streamlined applications" need to be actively communicated to the candidates in the job advertisements.
- *An elaborated user guidance through the application process is essential for usability.* Candidates need to keep control and keep track of each step in the application process. Due to the specific nature of mobile usage situations, the users must be able to interrupt and continue the application at any time.

Additional requirements for the implementation of a mobile application process need to be considered depending on the respective platform. Job openings published on corporate websites with singular candidate contacts might require a different approach for implementation compared to job portals with cross-company job offerings and recurrent users. A "one-click-application" for example requires the candidate to initially upload standardized application documents to be able to quickly respond to new job alerts. Therefore, from a user perspective, a "one-click-application" is attractive only for job portals or large enterprises with a high number of open positions matching the candidate's qualification.

VI. Limitations

This study was based on a convenient sample and can therefore not be considered to be representative. The data was collected in the environment of media-affine students. Therefore, it can be assumed that the results represent an early adopter group rather than the larger majority of young talents. Another limitation results from this study's focus on the user requirements with regard to the frontend interface on the smartphone. This is a gross simplification of reality as most of today's job offers and online applications are interfaced with backend systems for candidate management. Further research is needed on an appropriate design of backend systems and processes to deduce the implications of the user requirements presented here.

Acknowledgment

The authors would like to thank V. Hähnel, E. Haupt, J. Huth, N. Iwanowski, and L. Pfeifer for contributing to this research paper by supporting the data collection and app prototyping.

References

[1] GSMA, 2016, The Mobile Economy 2016. https://gsmaintelligence.com/research/?file=97928efe09cdba2864cdcf1ad1a2f58c&download, retrieved: 14.03.2016.

[2] J. Dischler, 2015, Building for the next moment. http://adwords.blogspot.de/2015/05/building-for-next-moment.html, retrieved: 14.03.2016.

[3] S. Angeles, 2015, Google Gives Mobile-Friendly Sites a Boost in Search Ranking. http://www.businessnewsdaily.com/7808-google-search-ranking-mobile.html, retrieved: 14.03.2016.

[4] E. Marcotte, Responsive web design. A Book Apart, New York, 2014.

[5] S. Böhm and S. J. Niklas, "Mobile recruiting: Insights from a survey among German HR managers," SIGMIS-CPR '12 Proceedings of the 50th annual conference on Computers and People Research, Milwaukee, USA, May 31-June 02, 2012, pp. 117–122.

[6] S. Böhm, "Behavior and expectations of mobile job seekers: An industry study focusing on job boards," SIGMIS-CPR '13 Proceedings of the 2013 Annual Conference on Computers and People Research, Cincinnati, USA, May 30-June 01, 2013, pp. 105–110.

[7] H. Zhang, 2015, Mobilize to realize: Job seeker insights for mobile recruitment success. http://public.dhe.ibm.com/common/ssi/ecm/lo/en/low14307usen/LOW14307USEN.PDF?, retrieved: 15.03.2016.

[8] Jobvite, 2015, Job Seeker Nation Study. Inside the Mind of the Modern Job Seeker. http://web.jobvite.com/FY15_Website_JobSeekerNation_LP.html?utm_source=Website&utm_medium=PressRelease&utm_campaign=2015JobSeekerNation, retrieved: 14.03.2016.

[9] Careerbuilder, 2015, 2015 Candidate Behavior U.S. Job-Seeker Data. http://b2b.careerbuilder.com/l/27812/ior-Report---US-JOB-SEEKER-pdf/7t7gk, retrieved: 14.03.2016.

[10] Careerbuilder, 2015, 2015 Candidate Behavior Germany Job-Seeker Data. http://b2b.careerbuilder.com/l/27812/eport---GERMANY-JOB-SEEKER-pdf/7nwgh, retrieved: 14.03.2016.

[11] S. Pande and N. Gomes, "Leveraging Mobile Devices for Human Resource Information Systems," Int'l J. of Business Information Systems 20, 1, pp. 23–40, 2015.

[12] S. Madan and K. Vasanth, "Mobile Recruitment - A Cutting or a Bleeding Edge…?," Int'l Journal of Management, IT and Engineering 3, 9, pp. 228–241, 2013.

[13] A. Zaheera, N. Khan, and C. B. Senthilkumar, "E-Recruitment: Criteria for its Effectiveness and Modern Trends," Int'l Journal of Business Administration and Management Research 1, 3, pp. 10–14, 2015.

[14] A. Eckhardt, S. Laumer, C. Maier, and T. Weitzel, "The transformation of people, processes, and IT in e-recruiting," Employee Relations 36, 4, pp. 415–431, 2014.

[15] S. J. B. Niklas and S. Strohmeier, "Exploring the Impact of Usefulness and Enjoyment on Mobile Service Acceptance: A Comparative Study," 2011 44th Hawaii Int'l Conference on System Sciences (HICSS 2011), pp. 1–10.

[16] S. J. Niklas and S. Böhm, "Applying Mobile Technologies for Personnel Recruiting. An Analysis of User-sided Acceptance Factors," Int'l Journal of eBusiness and eGoverment Studies 3, 1, pp. 169–178, 2011.

[17] S. J. Niklas, "Mobile IS Success in Personnel Marketing: A Consumer-based Analysis of Quality and Perceived Value," SIGMIS-CPR '11 Proceedings of the 49th SIGMIS annual conference on Computer personnel research, May 19-21, 2011, 2011, pp. 91–95.

[18] S. Böhm, W. Jäger, S. Meurer, and S. J. Niklas, "Optimizing the Usability of Mobile Job Advertisements: A Multi-Method Approach," Int'l Journal on Advances in Intelligent Systems 7, 1&2, pp. 257–266, 2014.

[19] S. Böhm, W. Jäger, S. Meurer, U. Rust, and W. Achilles, "Mobile Recruiting and Video Enhanced Job Advertisements: A Case Study Analysis within a German Job Portal," Proceedings of The Eighth International Conference on Advances in Human-Oriented and Personalized Mechanisms, Technologies, and Services, November 15-20, 2015, Barcelona, Spain, pp. 80–85.

[20] T. Lowdermilk, User-centered design. O'Reilly Media, Inc, Sebastopol, CA, 2013.

[21] S. Böhm and B. Igler, 2013, "A Tool-based Approach for Structuring Feedback for User Interface Evaluations of Mobile Applications," MobileHCI 2013 Workshop on Prototyping to Support the Interaction Designing in Mobile Application Development, pp. 1–4.

[22] S. Bochmann and T. Ritz, Prototyping tools for mobile applications. Steinbeis-Ed, Stuttgart, 2013.

[23] S. Ginsburg, Designing the iPhone user experience. A user-centered approach to sketching and prototyping iPhone apps. Addison-Wesley, Upper Saddle River, NJ, 2011.

[24] M.-S. Kim and C. Kim, "A Methodology for the Development of New Mobile Application Service Concepts," Advanced Science Letters 20, 1, pp. 336–339, 2014.

[25] Proto.io, Prototypes that feel real. https://proto.io/, retrieved: 05.04.2016.

PROFRAME: A Prototyping Framework for Mobile Enterprise Applications

Matthias Jurisch, Bodo Igler, Stephan Böhm

Faculty of Design – Computer Science – Media
RheinMain University of Applied Sciences
Wiesbaden, Germany
Email: {matthias.jurisch,bodo.igler,stephan.boehm}@hs-rm.de

***Abstract*—The rise of mobile device dissemination over the last few years and their short product life cycles require developers of enterprise applications to adapt to this situation. While the development of consumer apps is supported by many tools and processes, these can not be easily adapted to enterprise needs. Therefore, new process models for Mobile Enterprise Application development are required. In this paper, we present an approach based on Software Product Lines and Design Science Research that gathers information in the form of patterns from existing projects to ease the development of new applications. This information contains data from a user, organizational and technical perspective. The approach is currently a work in progress but will be further developed in the future.**

Keywords*–*Mobile Enterprise Applications; Design Science Research; Software Product Lines; User-centered Design; Prototyping; Pattern Inventories.

I. INTRODUCTION

Over the last few years, a rise in the dissemination of mobile devices could be observed. The development of applications for these devices is characterized by short product life cycles and high expectations regarding the usability of applications. On the other hand, development culture in large enterprises is often founded on precise specification and heavy-weight processes. Large enterprises usually have several requirements concerning compliance, security, linking to legacy back-end-applications and adherence to corporate design guidelines whereas in the mobile consumer market, these problems are not necessarily considered. In the mobile consumer market, new processes and concepts have been developed, which do not suit the needs for user-centric application development in large enterprises. Therefore, tools and approaches for *Mobile Enterprise Application* (MEA) development are required.

In this paper, we present a Prototyping Framework for Mobile Enterprise Applications (PROFRAME) containing a tool and process model using a prototyping approach that suits mobile enterprise applications. This process uses *structured and formal modeling* of application artifacts to support prototyping and takes organizational aspects of software projects into account. The process itself is based on the established methodology *design science research.*

The paper is organized as follows: Scientific work related to our project is presented in Section II. Our approach is described in Section III. Preliminary results are presented in Section IV. A conclusion and outlook are given in Section V.

II. RELATED WORK

According to [1] and [2], many enterprises still lack experience concerning the development of MEAs. While there are no established process models for MEA development, first research approaches for process models can be found in related literature. Dugerdil [3] presents an approach for transforming enterprise applications to mobile applications. An instrumentation framework that tries to ease the maintenance of MEAs is proposed in [4]. The management perspective of this problem is also represented in literature. Badami [5] examines this aspect from an organizational viewpoint and proposed the concentration of MEA development into "Mobile Centers of Excellence" that concentrate the competences of mobile experts inside enterprises.

The previously mentioned processes can be supported by tools. Existing prototyping tools (Kony, Verivo, Akula, SAP Mobile Platform) allow rapid prototyping. These tools can not always be used in MEA-contexts, since they are focused on predefined use cases or the integration of existing enterprise products.

No processes or tools that specifically support the development of MEAs can be found in literature or in practice. Therefore, new approaches are required that take the characteristics of MEAs into account. Central questions that need to be answered are how the approach can take the specifics of MEAs into account and how the approach can decrease the time and effort for development. These questions could be answered through reuse of artifacts from existing MEA projects. Frameworks or approaches focusing on the inventory and reuse of technical components, user interface patterns or organizational aspects can not be found in literature or practice. Especially organizational aspects are not represented in mainly software-focused work.

III. APPROACH

Our hypothesis is that in a pool of MEA projects, there are some artifacts or patterns from different domains (organizational, technical and UI design aspects) that can be reused in future projects. The idea of our approach is to analyze existing completed MEA-projects and extract these patterns and artifacts from them. Patterns are stored in a knowledge base that allows efficient searching and semantic modeling. This knowledge base can then be used for new MEA-projects that can reuse components of earlier MEAs.

The knowledge base will contain knowledge from (at least) three perspectives. These perspectives are a user-centric view on the application including its UI design, technical aspects concerning the platform and structure of the application and an organizational viewpoint on the project. This can be used to aid the reuse of artifacts from other projects. Reusing components from earlier work efficiently can help concentrating on aspects like user-centricity and reduce resources required to carry out the project. This would make it easier for MEA-development to catch up with consumer app development.

To efficiently execute this process, a tool is required. The tool will enable the creation of new patterns, entering existing projects including the usage of patterns into the knowledge base and creating new projects, as well as a UI prototype from a wireframe-like UI editor. The information for new projects can then be used to find relevant existing projects including information about potential reusable artifacts and knowledge from existing projects. An example for the UI for entering information regarding new patterns is shown in Fig. 1. For each pattern, a name and a description (1), specific properties (2) and an image for graphical representation (3) can be added. If the pattern is a *UI pattern* (4), the image can be used inside the tool's UI editor during the creation of a new project.

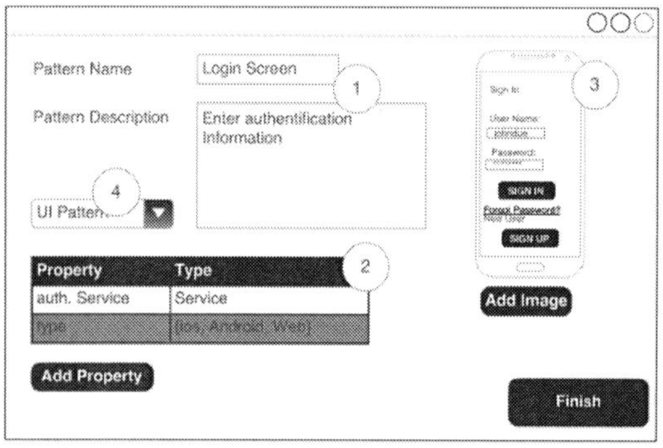

Figure 1. Prototype for Tool UI

Our approach combines aspects from the fields of software engineering, semantic technologies, IT-management and User-Centered Design. We divided the problem into four sub-problems, where we apply knowledge from these fields. The subproblems are:

1) identification of reusable software components in existing software,
2) adequate description, filing and semantic linking of information regarding these software components,
3) representing non-technical aspects in the knowledge base,
4) development of a tool that aides the application of the process with a high usability and
5) a process for a continuous construction of a suitable inventory.

To identify reusable components in software systems (problem 1), a detailed analysis of the software features and artifacts is required. Similar problems are addressed by *Software Product Lines*, which are discussed in Section III-A. Existing collections of reusable components exist as collections of *User Interface Design Patterns*, which is described in Section III-B. Creating an adequate modeling framework (problems 2,3 and 4) requires modern approaches from *Model driven Software Development* (Section III-C). To support interlinking of information from several domains and inference of new knowledge, *Semantic Technologies* (Section III-D) can provide useful technical concepts. For the development process (problem 5), domain feedback and inclusion of existing knowledge is important. These aspects are addressed in the area of *Design Science Research*, which is described in Section III-E.

A. *Software Product Lines*

Software Product Lines (SPL) [6] is an approach from the field of software engineering. Its main target is to ease the production of software variants while systematically reusing software components. The foundation for SPL is a catalog of artifacts. In production, these artifacts can be combined and adapted to produce new software variants.

SPL can contribute greatly to our approach. Product-feature trees that contain the features of a software product line, can be reused to describe features of MEAs in the knowledge base in our problem context. But SPL cannot be directly applied to our problem setting. SPL typically starts from scratch to develop a software product line, while our approach extracts patterns and artifacts from existing MEAs. Also, switching to a full-fledged SPL-approach would require a great deal of time and high effort, which is problematic for enterprises in the MEA-field given the dynamic market. Aspects that could be reused from SPL are Product-feature trees as well as reusable software components.

B. *User Interface Design Pattern Libraries*

Usage of patterns is state of the art in software engineering, especially for technical aspects of software design (e.g. [7]). Nowadays, patterns are used in all areas of software engineering. For our problem domain, user interface design pattern libraries [8] can provide an important contribution.

Besides pattern libraries for conventional desktop software, there are also pattern libraries for mobile applications (e.g. [9]). To use these concepts in the field of MEAs, they need to be transferred to the enterprise context. Relating these patterns to other system artifacts is important for the application of these concepts, too. Then, these patterns can be reused for prototyping, which could include the usage of technical system artifacts.

C. *Model Driven Software Development*

In Software Engineering, models are used for specification, analysis and design of systems. The models usually contain information about the structure or behavior of the described system and provide some kind of meaning (semantic) for this information. *Model Driven Software Development* (MDSD) deals with the automated generation of software components from these models [10]. This can help integrate domain experts into the development process who are not experienced with software development. The generated components can then be integrated into manually created software.

In the context of our problem domain, adequate models for describing system artifacts and software components including their dependencies and organizational aspects of the corresponding software projects are of importance. Whether existing modeling languages can be used to fulfill these requirements or a new language needs to be designed has to be examined.

D. *Semantic Technologies*

For the modeling, semantic modeling technologies based on ontologies can be used. Ontologies are defined as an "explicit specification of a conceptualization" [11]. Ontologies provide a mechanism to represent concepts and the relations between them. The semantics of the representation allow the inference of new knowledge from the ontology. Tim Berners-Lee and others proposed the semantic web, a technical approach to applying ontology-based technologies to the web

[12]. The semantic web is especially useful for interlinking information from different domains.

An excerpt from an example ontology is shown in Fig. 2. The excerpt shows a hierarchy of concepts. The concept `'App Component'` is a sub-concept of `owl:Thing`, which represents all concepts. `'App Component'` itself has several sub-concepts. In addition to the simple taxonomic structure shown in the example, ontologies support the definition of relations between instances of concepts and restrictions to these relations.

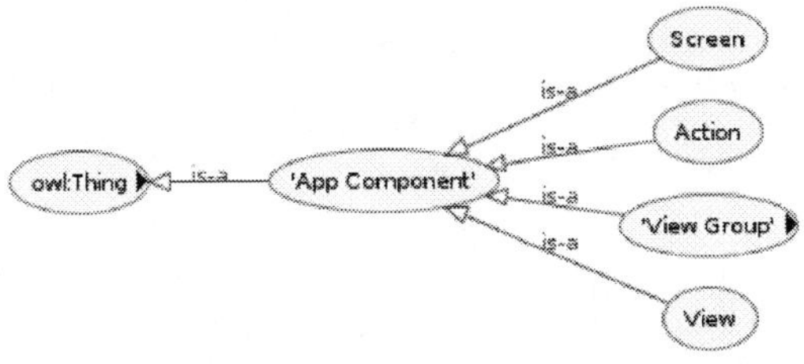

Figure 2. Example Ontology

In our approach, semantic web technologies will be used to provide a knowledge base that contains project information from completed MEA projects. The natural support for interlinking data from different domains will be useful when integrating the data from a user centric view, a technical artifact standpoint and an organizational perspective. These schemes can then be connected via so-called mapping ontologies. The separate development of ontologies for different domains might help bootstrapping the approach.

E. Design Science Research

Design Science Research (DSR) was proposed by Hevner et. al. [13]. It unites concepts from behavioral and design science in a cyclic model. The objective of this process is to improve the application domain by creating new artifacts (products and processes). The starting point of the process originates from requirements that stem from the application domain. Every artifact created in the process is validated against these requirements in the *relevance cycle*. Field tests are used to confirm that a created artifact meets the domain requirements. The artifacts are created in the *design cycle*, which also evaluates the artifacts based on the requirements. This cycle is the core of the process. The *rigor cycle* provides access to and updates a knowledge base that is used in the design cycle.

The DSR-model can be applied in two ways: The process model and other artifacts can be seen as artifacts of the DSR-process. Hence, DSR can be seen as the process model for our future research. The other perception would include the DSR-process into the created process model, where MEA-artifacts are seen as artifacts in the sense of DSR. The knowledge base can be structured as an ontology and the knowledge base used in the rigor cycle.

IV. Preliminary Results

Preliminary results for the usage of the tool and its integration into the app development process and the tools architecture were found. The concept for usage is described in Section IV-A and the tool's architecture is presented in Section IV-B.

A. Tool Usage Concept

There are two different modes when using the tool. The first mode is entering existing, finished projects into the tool's knowledge base. In this mode, the user can enter several details regarding the project. These details are separated into three views: the user-centric view of the application, including requirements and UI design, the technical viewpoint and an organizational perspective on the project.

The UI perspective contains details regarding the flow of screens and is represented in a wireframe-like editor. The user can annotate theses screens with patterns (see Fig. 1) to add more details to the knowledge base. The technical perspective can be used to specify, among others, a development platform, a deployment platform, used services and related artifacts. The IT-management perspective can be used to enter information regarding the organizational aspects of the project like the process model used, costs, development time and other organizational aspects. The information can be entered through form-based editors using attribute-value pairs.

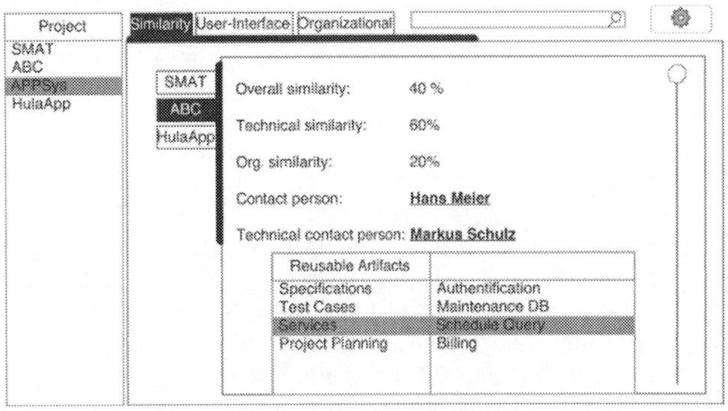

Figure 3. Screen Prototype for similarity View

The second mode allows the user to create a new project. The user can fill out the information that is known about the project with the same forms that are used to enter existing projects. The user can then open a similarity view that shows similarity scores for existing projects. A prototype for that view is depicted in Fig. 3. The user can see different similarity scores for the different perspectives as well as contact persons for different aspects of the project. In the bottom of the view is a table that contains reusable artifacts that can be filtered by categories. Moreover, the user can generate a prototype from the wireframe-like UI editor, which is not shown in this paper.

B. Tool Architecture

The tool's architecture is depicted in Fig. 4 as a Fundamental Modeling Concepts diagram. The two modes of operation presented in Section IV-A are both executed by the *PROFRAME User*. The *Project Participant* uses an ontology editor to edit the structure of the knowledge base and adds the initial project data concerning the technical, business- and user-related aspects. The ontologies are connected through a mapping ontology that relates the concepts from the different ontologies to each other, using the natural interlinking support of ontologies. Ontologies can also ease the variability of the knowledge base. From the ontology, an MDSD-Framework can generate the *PROFRAME Project Tool*, which can then be used by the *PROFRAME User*.

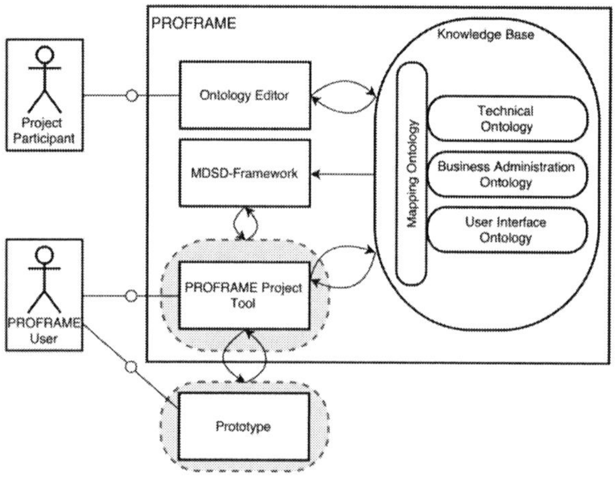

Figure 4. Tool Architecture

The *PROFRAME User* can enter the project data for a new project into the *PROFRAME Project tool*, which is also represented as the content of the ontology. The user enters data regarding desired process model, platform, etc. A wireframe that uses existing patterns can also be used as input. From the wireframe, the tool can generate a prototype that can be used to demonstrate the capabilities of the planned application to customers. To further plan the project, the user can use the screen shown in Fig. 3, which can be used to, e.g., find contact persons with relevant information and potential reusable artifacts. The *PROFRAME project tool* is also responsible for computing the similarities between planned and existing projects to be shown in a similarity view reusing approaches from the field of recommendation systems for software engineering. An implementation could use case based reasoning, where the similarities between cases can be computed using word similarity in the descriptions of the projects, similar to the work presented in [14]. Using structural similarity measures could also be of use. Another promising strategy for finding similar projects is the use of rule-based recommender systems [15], that explicitly state the relation between properties of the projects.

V. Conclusion and Outlook

In this paper, we have presented an approach to tackle the difficulties of mobile enterprise application development. Our approach combines methods from the domains of software product lines, user interface design pattern libraries, model driven software development, semantic technologies and design science research to improve the development process. The approach has the advantages that it allows early prototyping and high reuse of existing artifacts. Therefore, it can lead to reduced costs for MEA projects. But most importantly, the approach organizes the knowledge from different MEA projects. The approach could prevent the loss of knowledge, when employees leave the company or are transfered to other positions. This could also reduce costs for companies employing this approach. Also, the approach could ease communication between teams inside the company.

In the future, we plan to implement our approach with an industry partner that uses mobile centers of excellence to evaluate and improve it. User motivation including the perceived usefulness and ease of use of the approach will be central to the evaluation. The outcome of the process will be a pattern inventory, a modeling language, a prototyping tool and a cost-benefit analysis of the overall approach. Also, our approach can lead to new scientific results on how to represent data regarding software development projects that take a technical, business-related and user-centric perspective into account. A process based on design science research for MEAs could be another interesting outcome. Another research question is whether the prototyping aspect of the process can improve the user-centricity of the resulting MEAs which will also be evaluated in the future.

References

[1] A. Giessmann, K. Stanoevska-Slabeva, and B. de Visser, "Mobile enterprise applications–current state and future directions," in System Science (HICSS), 2012 45th Hawaii International Conference on, Jan 2012, pp. 1363–1372, Jan 2012.

[2] Gartner, "Gartner says demand for enterprise mobile apps will outstrip available development capacity five to one," https://www.gartner.com/newsroom/id/3076817, website [retrieved: June, 2016], 2015.

[3] P. Dugerdil, "Architecting mobile enterprise app: A modeling approach to adapt enterprise applications to the mobile," in Proceedings of the 2013 ACM Workshop on Mobile Development Lifecycle, ser. MobileDeLi '13. New York, NY, USA: ACM, 2013, pp. 9–14, 2013.

[4] M. Pistoia and O. Tripp, "Integrating security, analytics and application management into the mobile development lifecycle," in Proceedings of the 2Nd International Workshop on Mobile Development Lifecycle, ser. MobileDeLi '14. New York, NY, USA: ACM, 2014, pp. 17–18, 2014.

[5] S. A. Badami and J. Sathyan, "micE Model for Defining Enterprise Mobile Strategy," Int. J. on Recent Trends in Engineering and Technology,, vol. 10, no. 1, p. 9, Jan 2014.

[6] K. Pohl, G. Böckle, and F. J. v. d. Linden, Software Product Line Engineering: Foundations, Principles and Techniques. Secaucus, NJ, USA: Springer-Verlag New York, Inc., 2005.

[7] F. Buschmann, R. Meunier, H. Rohnert, P. Sommerlad, and M. Stal, Pattern-Oriented Software Architecture - Volume 1: A System of Patterns. Wiley Publishing, 1996.

[8] M. Welie, G. C. Veer, and A. Eliëns, Tools for Working with Guidelines: Annual Meeting of the Special Interest Group. London: Springer London, 2001, ch. Patterns as Tools for User Interface Design, pp. 313–324, 2001.

[9] "Mobile patterns," http://www.mobile-patterns.com/, website [retrieved: June, 2016], 2016.

[10] T. Stahl, M. Voelter, and K. Czarnecki, Model-Driven Software Development: Technology, Engineering, Management. John Wiley & Sons, 2006.

[11] T. R. Gruber, "Toward principles for the design of ontologies used for knowledge sharing," Int. J. Hum.-Comput. Stud., vol. 43, no. 5-6, pp. 907–928, Dec. 1995.

[12] T. Berners-Lee, J. Hendler, and O. Lassila, "The semantic web," Scientific American, vol. 284, no. 5, pp. 34–43, May 2001.

[13] A. R. Hevner, "A three cycle view of design science research," Scandinavian Journal of Information Systems, pp. 87–92, 2007.

[14] P. Gomes, F. C. Pereira, P. Paiva, N. Seco, P. Carreiro, J. Ferreira, and C. Bento, "Selection and Reuse of Software Design Patterns Using CBR and WordNet," SEKE'03, 2003.

[15] F. Palma, H. Farzin, Y. G. Guéhéneuc, and N. Moha, "Recommendation system for design patterns in software development: An DPR overview," RSSE 2012, pp. 1–5, 2012.

Using Mobile Geographical Information System for Biomass Waste Management

Valentim Realinho, Miguel Belém
Polytechnic Institute of Portalegre
Portalegre, Portugal
e-mail: vrealinho@estgp.pt, miguel.belem@ipportalegre.pt

***Abstract*—Land cover maps are one of the main data sources used to assess the availability of biomass residues. Mobile Geographic Information Systems can help field work providing spatial data including map browsing, query and collecting field information. However, the large amount of data undergoing processing, creates challenges for its use on mobile devices, because of the typical constraints of these devices. In this paper, it is presented a mobile solution that is able to handle efficiently large amount of spatial data, which is part of a platform for biomass waste management.**

Keywords-Mobile geographic information system; geovisualization; mobile computing; biomass waste; field work.

I. Introduction

Almost 13% of the renewable energy consumed around the world in 2006 derived from biomass [1]. The biomass resources are of different types and its availability varies geographically widely. On the other hand, the biomass resources exhibit different power generation characteristics and have to be transported to power plants. These demands have created opportunities for the use of decision support systems based on spatial information that utilize advanced mapping, mobile field-based applications and Location Based Systems (LBS). These systems can be used for the selection of places for bioenergy projects or in the assessment and mapping of biomass residues and the estimation of transport costs to existent or proposed power plants.

Land cover maps are one of the main data sources which feed those systems [2]. They are produced using mainly orthorectified imagery from satellites, aircraft, Unmanned Aerial Vehicles (UAV) and also information collected in field in a high cost process. Because of this, the land cover maps are often out of date due to natural causes or human intervention, which could represent a problem in some uses.

A geographic information system (GIS) has the ability to handle and process land cover maps, enabling users to view and analyze geospatial data with ease. A GIS is an expensive investment and data intensive system that must handle a large amount of data. The use of mobile GIS tools can provide information for real time analysis and data collection in the field. However, condensing GIS information for mobile computing, is a complex task due to typical constraints of this types of devices.

In this work, it is presented a mobile tool that is part of a platform that allow the biomass waste management which include data from Alto Alentejo (Portugal) and Extremadura (Spain) regions in a total of 3.230.323 ha registered in the platform.

In addition to this introductory section, this paper is organized as follows: Section 2 presents a summary of key technologies and projects in the field of GIS and mobile GIS. Section 3 presents some topics concerned the processing of land cover maps. Section 4 deals with the technical approach and finally in Section 5, we present the main conclusions.

II. Related Work

Modern GIS architectures rely on a client/server model [3] in a distributed environment based on a GIS Server and clients that can be desktop, web or mobile applications. A GIS Server share geospatial data and functions, while client subsystems act as consumers through a set of interfaces. The Open Geospatial Consortium (OGC) provides a blueprint for implementing these interfaces in a Service Oriented Architecture (SOA) [4]. These interfaces support interoperable solutions and empower technology developers to make complex spatial information and services accessible and useful with all kinds of applications. They are categorized according to the type of data they provide and the most important are the Web Map Service (WMS), the Web Feature Service (WFS) and the Web Coverage Service (WCS). The Web Map Service provides a simple HTTP interface for requesting geo-registered map images from one or more distributed geospatial databases [5]. A WMS request produces complete maps, rendered at the server and transmitted as images to the client that can be displayed in a browser application. The Web Feature Service provides an interface allowing requests for geographical features across the web using platform-independent calls [6]. It supplies individual features, encoded as vectors, selected from the underlying spatial database, to be rendered at the client side. The Web Coverage Service offers multi-dimensional coverage data for access over the Internet [7]. Unlike WMS, WCS provides only non-interactive data access. Besides commercial products, there is a number of open source projects, such as MapServer, GeoServer or GeoNetwork, which provide OGC compliant servers for sharing geospatial data, suitable for the development of custom applications.

The data tier of a GIS Server include spatial database servers that store geo-data and retrieve data according to client or application server business logic. Products like PostGIS, SpatiaLite, Oracle Spatial and ArcSDE, are examples of spatial database servers. They supports spatial and non-spatial data, besides common geographic file formats such as Shapefiles, GeoTiff, Keyhole Markup Language (KML), Geography Markup Language (GML), Scalable Vector Graphics (SVG), GeoRSS or GeoJSON.

Mobile devices have a lack of resources when compared with a desktop computer that represent constraints to handle massive amount of data such in GIS. There are form factor, storage, computing, battery and network issues that need to be addressed. Projects like the ones presented in [3][8][9], attempt to introduce mobile computing as an aid for field work and data collection.

The mobile tool presented in this article implements a location-based system that provides information on the availability of biomass and its potential to produce energy, still allowing the correction of spatial data in the field. To make this possible, in an efficiently way, spatial data are preprocessed in a server and only then made available to the mobile device.

III. PROCESSING LAND COVER MAPS

The land cover maps we used (Alto Alentejo-Portugal and Extremadura-Spain), totalize an area of 3.230.323 ha. This area is represented as over 78.000 polygons and multi-polygons, which describe a particular agricultural or forest residues within the boundaries of the municipality. This create a geospatial dataset of over 8 million data points, and represents a challenge especially for use in field work through mobile devices.

The analysis of the land cover maps, revels a huge number of polygons and multi-polygons that can be optimized through the use of dissolve operations. Dissolve is an aggregation process in which a new map feature is created by merging adjacent polygons that have a common value for a specified attribute, in this case the same biomass family and the same parish or municipality. Fig. 1 illustrates how a dissolve operation work.

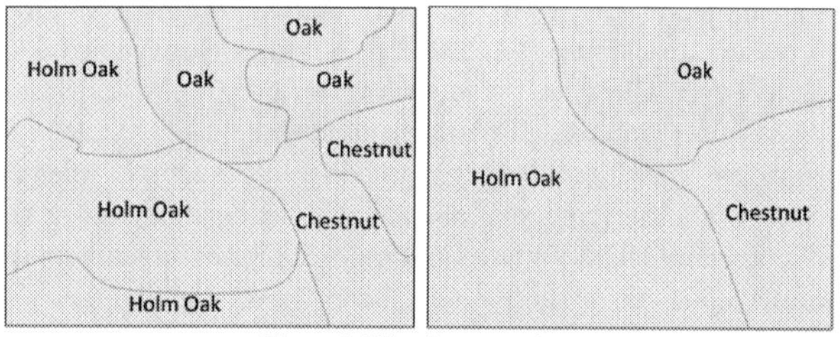

Figure 1. Dissolve operation.

With this, we reduced the number of polygons in 97% (from 78.854 to 2.339), and the number of data points in 35% (from 8.031.020 to over 5.216.195). The resulting geospatial dataset was then loaded into the server with metadata, which include, among others, the estimation of existent biomass residues and the determination of electrical generation potential according with the model defined in [2].

IV. TECHNICAL APPROACH

The system architecture is illustrated in Fig. 2. This architecture consists of a server that responds to the project domain [10]. We use GeoServer with PostGIS which share its data through WMS and WFS standards.

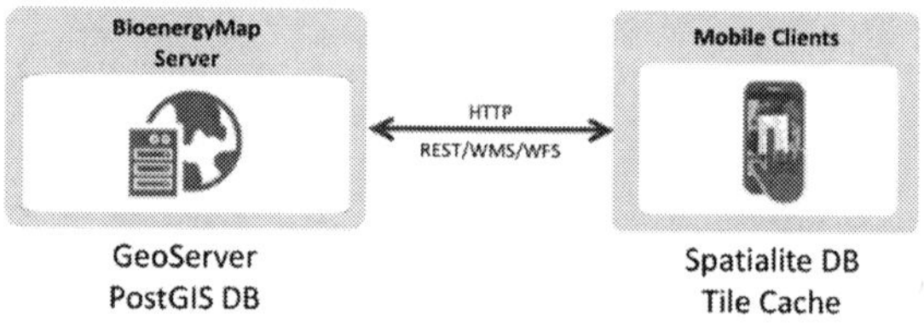

Figure 2. System architecture.

The mobile clients (Android smartphones or tablets) show spatial data using Google Maps overlaid with tiles received from GeoServer which represent the layers concerning a particular feature like biomass families, production, energy potential or cover type among others (Fig. 3a and Fig. 3b). A tile overlay (or tile layer) is a collection of images that are displayed on top of the base map.

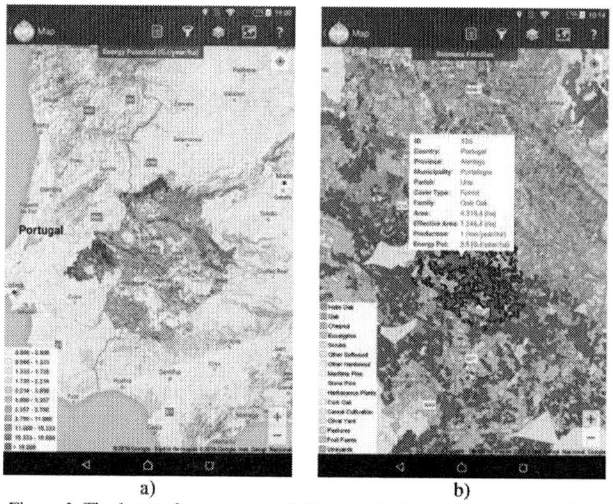

a) b)

Figure 3. The layer of energy potential (a) and the layer of biomass families with a multi-polygon selected represented Cork Oak of Urra parish (b).

In a field work environment, the mobile client works in a setting where the connection to the server is unstable or slow. For this reason, mobile clients has an implemented mechanism for caching map tiles received from the server.

We use Spatialite (a spatial extension to SQLite) in the mobile clients. The database is synchronized with the server and maintain the same information for offline use.

Besides the map, the mobile client also allows the visualization of spatial data in a table fashion.

V. Conclusions

In this paper, we present a solution for the use of a mobile GIS which is part of a platform for biomass waste management. This solution can help field work providing spatial data including map browsing, query and collecting field information.

Currently we have registered information from Alto Alentejo (Portugal) and Extremadura (Spain) regions in a total of more than 3,2 millions hectares registered in the platform. The evaluation performed proved that the solution is able to handle efficiently this large amount of data.

The mobile application is free available in Google Play and all the platform in [10].

Acknowledgment

This work was cofounded by FEDER under program POCTEP, priority axis 1 (Promoting competitiveness and employment promotion - project 0606_MITTIC_4_E).

References

[1] V. Cigolotti, "Biomass and Waste as Sustainable Resources," in Fuel Cells in the Waste-to-Energy Chain, London: Springer London, 2012, pp. 23–44.

[2] G. Lourinho and P. Brito, "Assessment of biomass energy potential in a region of Portugal (Alto Alentejo)," Energy, vol. 81, pp. 189–201, 2015.

[3] N. Jajac, D. Stojanovic, B. Predic, and D. Rancic, "Efficient replication of geospatial data for mobile GIS in field work," in 2013 11th International Conference on Telecommunications in Modern Satellite, Cable and Broadcasting Services (TELSIKS), 2013, vol. 02, pp. 393–396.

[4] Open Geospatial Consortium, "OGC Standards and Supporting Documents." [Online]. Available from: http://www.opengeospatial.org/standards 2016.06.15.

[5] Open Geospatial Consortium, "Web Map Service." [Online]. Available from: http://www.opengeospatial.org/standards/wms 2016.06.15.

[6] Open Geospatial Consortium, "Web Feature Service." [Online]. Available from: http://www.opengeospatial.org/standards/wfs 2016.06.15.

[7] Open Geospatial Consortium, "Web Coverage Service." [Online]. Available from: http://www.opengeospatial.org/standards/wcs 2016.06.15.

[8] A. Huynh and A. Y.-M. Lin, "Mobile Analysis of Large Temporal Datasets for Exploration and Discovery," in 2013 Digital Heritage International Congress (DigitalHeritage), 2013, vol. 2, pp. 535–538.

[9] M. M. Elwakil, R. F. Ibrahim, and H. A. Hefny, "New Architecture for Mobile GIS Cloud Computing," Int. J. Adv. Res. Comput. Commun. Eng., vol. 4, no. 10, pp. 1–7, 2015.

[10] C3i/IPP, "Bioenergy Map - Plataforma de Geestão de Biomassa," 2014. [Online]. Available from: www.bioenergymap.pt 2016.06.15.

A Citizen-centric Public Sector

Why citizen centricity matters and how to obtain it

Lasse Berntzen, Marius Rode Johannessen and Ansgar Ødegård
Department of Business and Management
University College of Southeast Norway
Kongsberg, Norway
emails: {lasse.berntzen, marius.johannessen, ansgar.odegard}@hbv.no

Abstract—**The paper discusses the concept of a citizen-centric public sector. Citizen centricity is often promoted in policy papers and political speeches, but is often overlooked in practice. Reasons are discussed, and practical examples are shown, to show failures and success stories. Information and communication technology may be a significant measure to enhance citizen centricity. The latest digital agenda of the Norwegian government emphasizes the use of information and communication technology to make a simpler everyday life and increase productivity. The agenda is ambitious, and the paper discusses some possible pitfalls and how to overcome them.**

Keywords - citizen centricity; eGovernement; digital agenda; organizational identity.

I. Introduction

This paper discusses citizen centricity in the public sector. A citizen-centric public sector implies putting the citizens in the center and building services around the citizen. Now, some readers would think "This is obvious, why write a paper about it"? But the fact is that the public sector is often implementing services that are not favorable to the citizens. Some reasons are:

- The public sector thinks about its internal efficiency, not taking into account the additional effort required by the users to achieve this efficiency.
- The public sector is complex and it is not able simplify the complexity for its users. The citizens see a lot of disconnected government entities and have to navigate by themselves.

Berntzen [1] showed the increasing government awareness of citizen centricity rooted in "New Public Management". The government should see citizens as customers and provide the same service level as experienced when dealing with private companies.

In November 2005, the UK Presidency of EU held a Ministerial Conference in Manchester. The adopted declaration from the conference [2] moved citizen centricity high on the political agenda. Based on the declaration, Blakemore et al. [3] were asked by the European Commission eGovernment Unit to do a two-year study on citizen-centric eGovernment. The project, called cc:eGov, conducted a number of workshops and produced a set of "think papers" to discuss different aspects of citizen-centric eGovernment. The final outcome of the project was a handbook [4]. The study did not emphasize user involvement in the development of services, but was more concerned with transformation of government to be more attentive to the needs and wishes of the citizens.

The European Commission also initiated other projects to explore citizen-centric eGovernment, e.g., OneStopGov [5]. The project was started in January 2006, and was a three year EU-funded research and development project that aimed at specifying, developing and evaluating a life-event oriented, all-inclusive, integrated, interoperable platform for online one-stop government.

The next Ministerial Conference on e-Government held in Lisbon, September 2007 declared that member states should "deliver eGovernment services that are easier to use and of benefit to all citizens by increasing user centricity, improving accessibility, convenience and user experience" [6].

User involvement in the whole lifecycle of eGovernment services received focus in 2010, with the establishment of the NET-EUCEN thematic network [7]. One of the activities of this network was to develop a framework for measuring user-centricity at all stages of the service lifecycle.

In spite of this increasing awareness, we experience that citizen centricity is more often talked about than implemented.

Citizen centricity is not primarily about technology, but technology can help building better services. Later we will show some examples of how government on different levels failed to consider the needs and wishes of citizens, but we will also show some success stories. Our examples are from Norway, and are partly based on our own experiences and discussions about citizen centricity. Our ambition was to find examples that are easy to explain and understand. We will then discuss the role of ICT in citizen centricity, and provide some guidance on how to use ICT in a meaningful way. We argue that citizen centricity is about mindset; public decision makers on all levels need to understand the importance of including citizens when developing services and products.

II. Methodology

The study was conducted following a qualitative research design and an interpretive epistemology. The objective of qualitative research is "understanding…by investigating the perspectives and behaviour of the people in these situations and the context within which they act" [8]. This fits well with our objective of discussing citizen centricity, as citizen centricity requires a thorough understanding of citizen needs and contexts.

The case study research design is suited for research on phenomena where the experiences and interpretations of the actors and the wider context are important factors [9]. Thus, we use example cases from Norwegian public sector as the empirical basis of our paper. We have chosen the cases as representative examples of the citizen-related challenges facing public sector modernization.

Data is analyzed using a model developed by Ødegård [10] – "*a learning model*" and shows how public organizations might respond to increasingly need for developing citizen-centric services. The model shows that decisions are often made and carried out because they provide legitimacy for the decision maker rather than effective solutions benefitting the citizens. Thus, effectiveness and efficiency are secondary factors when decisions are made. On the other hand, decision makers also tend to make decisions based solely on organizational culture hindering the organization members in realizing the «changing citizens need» – the focus of the culture is primarily on internal needs and professional technical service standards without paying particularly attention to changing external (citizens) needs without paying attention to changing stakeholder demands and expectations, like changing citizen needs. Thus, organizations seem captured by the culture and past traditions without paying sufficient attention to future needs and expectations from the citizens. In other words, the organizations might make decisions regarding citizen centricity within the cultural frame "*the way we have always done things around here*". We apply this model in order to test if this could be the reason why Norwegian public sector still struggles to become citizen-centric, even though several plans exist that state this as a primary objective.

III. Organizational Identity on the Move in Public Sector Organizations

The concept of organizational identity has received increased attention in the past decades. Albert and Whetten's [11] classical definition of organizational identity focuses on features such as central, distinctive and enduring as key elements of organizational identity. However, a more dynamic perspective on organizational identity is increasingly common. Organizational identity consists of an ongoing dynamics between culture and image [12] and thus emphasizing agency and the possibility for organizations to reconstruct their identity. However, this demands a long-term perspective and involvement of both internal and external stakeholders. Schultz and Hernes [13] offer a framework for how the past traditions connect to future aspirations and thus influencing identity construction – a temporal perspective on organizational identity. Accordingly, the time – the past, present and the future – constitutes organizational identity through tangled processes evolving in time.

Organizational identity is constructed through four processes of mirroring (in the mirror of others), reflecting (culture, embedded in history and traditions, meanings and understandings), expressing (the way culture is being expressed) and impressing (leave impression on others) [12]. Accordingly, organizational identity consists of the two concepts of image and culture. Culture represents the past, the roots and thus the core identity. Osborne [14] describes culture as the DNA (Deoxyribonucleic acid) of an organization. Radical organization transformation requires cultural change through behaviors, values and basic assumptions [15]. We consider culture change as crucial in order to develop an organization culture in accordance with a citizen-centric public sector culture in which the citizens are in the center of all activities.

Due to demands for transparency, the introduction of New Public Management and increasing stakeholder expectations there seems to be a need for public organizations to work purposely on the matter of reconstructing their identity. Organizations express themselves through identity claims, telling "who they are", "where they come from" and "who they are going to be" in the future. Thus, the past and the future are closely interconnected. However, as the cases reveal, there seem to be a lack of connection between the culture part of public organizational identity and the image part. It seems that public organizations give great attention to different activities and projects which are nearly exclusively connected to the past and existing culture. This is done without having taken into account how a citizen-centric organization ought to be organized in order to fulfil the increasing expectations from the citizens. On the other hand, the cases expose the opposite tendency of uncritical focus on legitimacy and image without necessarily connect the projects through involvement and engagement with the existing culture.

Two dysfunctions might occur when culture and images become disassociated [12]. When organizational identity is rooted nearly exclusively within the culture, a type of organizational narcissism might evolve, losing interest and support from external stakeholders. Accordingly, as shown in the cases, efforts of citizen centricity might fail due to overemphasizing of the past traditions and culture of the organization without really paying attention to the need and expectations of the citizens. On the other hand, when identity primarily is occupied with external stakeholder images and legitimacy, ignoring cultural heritage and the past, the risk of losing the sense of "who we are" and "where we come from" emerge. According to Hatch and Shultz [12], this is called hyper-adaption, or *"loss of culture"*. As shown in the cases, the efforts of citizen centricity might also fail due to overemphasizing on external stakeholder images and legitimacy. Thus, the organizations are occupied with gaining legitimacy, making an impression of being a citizen-centric public organization without necessarily emphasizing effectiveness, the needs and the expectations of the citizens.

Organizational culture is a conservative force within organizations, developed over time ensuring stability [15]. Thus, strong cultures seem hard to change. In an increasingly more turbulent and complex world there seems to be a need for organizations to develop flexibility and learning capabilities. Hence, a learning culture characterized by a stabilized flexibility seems crucial. A learning culture featured by processes of learning, adaption and flexibility might be a key for public organizations to meet increased complexity, transparency and expectations from both internal and external stakeholders. In order for public organizations to succeed in being a citizen-centric organization, we claim that developing a learning culture seems necessary. Otherwise a tendency of failures and lack of citizen centricity, which is showed in this paper probably, still will appear. We suggest that a strong learning culture will foster innovation and adaption to an increasingly more complex and dynamic world of stakeholders for public organizations.

IV. Examples of Being Non-citizen-centric

The following examples illustrate some of the typical problems of forgetting about the needs and wants of citizens. Each case illustrates a specific problem, and it has been the intention not to find pure information technology related examples, just because citizen centricity is relevant to all products and services delivered by the government.

A. The train sets the customers did not want.

In 2012, NSB, the Norwegian railroad operator (government owned) put 23 new train sets into service. The next day, customers started complaining about the seats being too narrow and uncomfortable. Due to massive complaints, NSB decided to change the seats for a cost of 51 million Norwegian crowns (almost 5 million Euro). The upgrade of the seats was finished in 2014 [16].

Figure 1. The Flirt train

The initial seat configuration was chosen to get maximum number of seats in each wagon. In a citizen-centric approach, the seat configuration would have been tested with real users. This case illustrates how important it is to involve users in the design and development of products and services.

B. Why do we need a driving license?

As a proof that you have passed the necessary test to show that you are a competent driver one needs a driver license. But, the driving license is a physical card, and you need to bring it with you. If you cannot produce your driving license while driving, you can get fined. But, when you produce the driving license, it is checked towards a database for validity. In fact, the driving license is just an ID, so why not accept any valid ID when in fact the validity is not in the card, but in the database. Fines bring money to the government, at the cost of irritated drivers that have to pay because they left their driving license at home or in their second car.

This example above shows how the governments, sometimes, are locking up in old ways of thinking, without taking into account the real needs and wants of the citizens.

United Kingdom had a driving license consisting of a photo card and a paper counterpart. The paper counterpart was abolished June 8th 2015 to save motorists' money, reduce red tape, and make sure that employers are not relying on potentially out-of-date paper [17]. The information is now stored online, and the holder may share this online information, e.g., with car rental companies that requires information about driving history [17].

C. The parking ticket machine

One of the authors was about to pay for parking in a municipal parking space, when he discovered a credit card left in the payment station. This payment station used the following routine: You put in the credit card, select parking time, get the parking ticket, and then remove the credit card. The card was returned to the unfortunate citizen. But, in later discussion we found that many users had the same experience. You are most concerned about getting the parking ticket, and therefore, it is easy to forget the card. In other parking stations, the sequence is different, you insert the card, select parking time, retrieve the credit card and then you get the ticket. Again, user testing with real users would have exposed this problem. In this case, it was not about internal efficiency or old ways, it was just about bad design.

The user experience (UX) of parking ticket machines has also been discussed by several bloggers on the Internet, e.g., [18].

There are probably enough other examples to prove the point that not all products and services are citizen-centric. The examples are just examples of what happens when citizen centricity is not taken seriously, and show the importance of involving citizen, not only when new services or products are planned, designed and developed, but also to accept that "what we always have done" is not necessarily in line with the needs of the users.

V. Examples of "Best Practice"

While there are many examples of lacking citizen-centricity, we have also seen several examples of services that are truly citizen-centric. Again, we have tried to find examples that are not technology-oriented:

A. Cancer Treatment Coordinator

One vulnerable group is patients diagnosed with cancer. Earlier, patients had to relate to many different persons and institutions. This may not be a big problem under normal circumstances, but when you get a possible terminal diagnosis, you may not be able to carry out the tasks you are expected to. The Special Health Services Act imposes a duty to appoint a coordinator for patients requiring "complex or long-term and coordinated services" [19]. Many hospitals have created designated cancer coordinator positions. The coordinators are responsible for coordinating the fastest possible assessment and treatment for patients, ensuring the provision of information about the treatment process for the patient and relatives at an early stage [19].

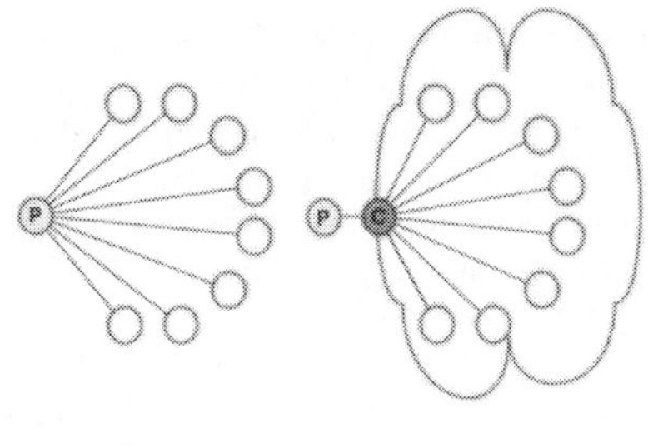

Figure 2. The coordinator hides the complex organization behind

Outside the hospitals, many municipalities have created their own designated cancer coordinators. The patient now only needs to relate to one single person who knows the system, the processes, and what needs to be done. The municipal coordinators collaborate with the hospital coordinator but also with other stakeholders to provide the best possible services for the patient [19].

B. *User-Controlled Personal Assistant*

Citizens with physical disabilities often need support to get around. The non-user centric approach is to tell the citizen that he/her will get help at certain times. "Lisa" is offered a walk in the park in the middle of the day, but what she really wants is to be with friend in a café on Friday evening. The user-managed personal assistant is the citizen-centric answer to such problems. The patient is given a certain number of hours a week, but the patient is in charge of how and when the hours are used. This empowers the patient.

Many municipalities have implemented user-controlled personal assistants as a service. In their political platform established on October 7th, 2013, the two parties of the current government agreed to establish access to user-controlled personal assistance as a right [20]. This was implemented in the Health and Rights Act on January 1st, 2015 [21].

These are two real life examples on citizen-centric approaches to service provision. What conclusions can we draw from these examples?

- The service is built around the user
- The user is empowered, and gets more control

We have chosen these examples on purpose. They are not related to ICT, and they show that citizen-centric is more than making better ICT solutions.

VI. CITIZEN CENTRICITY

It is now time to discuss the concept of citizen centricity in more detail. As we have already seen, citizen centricity is not obvious. The main idea is to learn from the users of products and services in order to make them better. This involves the users in design, development and implementation of the products and services. In order to do that, systematic collection of user input is needed. Users may and should be co-creators of the products and services, not just consumers. They may add their wishes and expectations, but also their competence.

We argue that citizen centricity is mainly about the collective mindset of public sector employees and decision makers. Citizens should be involved in all phases of product or service development. The user involvement should be sufficient, not superficial. It is necessary to pay close attention to wants and wishes in order to succeed.

Citizens can be involved on different levels. On the policy level, user organizations can speak on behalf of the users. At system level, some users can speak for the rest. And on the individual level each user speaks for him/herself. On this level we talk about customization of products and services.

A. *ICT and Citizen Centricity*

Most services provided by government on different levels are depending on human resources. Teachers teach our children, healthcare personnel take care of those with medical problems, and manual work is needed to maintain roads. But, ICT plays an increasing role in the service provision. The teachers are using ICT to communicate with parents, those with medical problems may book consultations online. Prescriptions are sent from the general practitioner (GP) to the pharmacy through electronic communication. Drivers may get updated information on road construction work through the Internet. Therefore, it is fair to say that electronic services play an important role in public service provision.

B. *Digital Agenda Norway*

In April 2016, the Norwegian government issued a white paper "Digital Agenda for Norway – ICT for a simpler everyday" [22]. One of the two key objectives of the white paper is a citizen-centric and effective public sector. It would be reasonable to say that the ambitions of the government are high.

The users (citizens, public and private entities and the voluntary sector), and their needs shall be the central starting point. Public services shall be seen as coordinated and complete, independent of which public sector entities are providing the services. The public sector should reuse information instead of asking users for information already acquired.

The government wants (among other things):

- Real user participation to ensure that users views and needs is taken care of in development of digital services.
- Stimulate more trials by using service design to contribute to more good user centric services.

VII. BARRIERS TO CITIZEN-CENTRICITY

Studies of barriers to eGovernment adoption often take a very broad or high level approach, by examining policy documents, interviewing project managers etc. While citizens are in focus, and citizen-centricity is promoted as a principle, existing research has put too little emphasis on the individual citizens' needs [23].

One exception is the study by Van Veenstra, Klievink and Janssen [24], who performed a literature review and also examined barriers in three case studies of eGovernment. They found barriers to be related to three broad areas: Governance, organizational issues and technical issues. Several of these are relevant when discussing citizen-centric government. Table 1 lists these issues, explains their relevance and their resolutions.

TABLE 1. BARRIERS TO EGOVERNMENT IMPLEMENTATION

Issue	Relevance	Resolution
Public sector structure, Fragmentation in service areas and/or decision-making responsibility	Public sector often structured so that responsibility for a specific area is scattered across several departments and government levels. This makes collaboration difficult.	Identify citizen needs in key areas, for example following life-cycle logic: "As a graduating student I need the following services"
Lack of communication/ collaboration/ coordination	Related to previous issue	Using citizen needs, identify which areas need collaboration
No relation/ alignment between organization and technology	Organization and IT areas are not cooperating fully, creating a gap between what is needed and what is possible.	Project teams should have at least one person who is equally proficient in technology and organization, acting as a bridge between the two.
Insufficient understanding of users	User needs are inferred, IT follows internal government logic rather than focusing on citizen needs	Involvement of citizens in planning, life-cycle based scenario planning. Searchable web sites.
Security and privacy not addressed	Lack of security and privacy makes many citizens hesitate to use the online service, and can lead to lack of trust in government, especially in countries where trust is low from before.	National eID-solutions needs to be in place, as well as clear and understandable privacy policies.
Lack of standards, Complexity and interoperability of legacy systems, Basic infrastructure underdeveloped	Legacy systems, different system vendors and a missing common infrastructure for eGovernment makes it difficult to create services that work across organizational silos, and also makes user interfaces complex and changing between one service and the next.	While difficult, government should strive for a common eGovernment infrastructure, life-cycle based services and a common, standardized user interface across all services.

While Table 1 lists important barriers, we need to extend this list with some observations from our own work on eGovernment projects.

A. Data quality and open data

Public sector managers are not very eager to share data, since they also feel responsible for the quality of the data shared. Government data has been collected over many years, and old data often has some quality issues. While the Agency for Public Management and eGovernment (DIFI) has set up a good portal for open data, the available data sets are often outdated or incomplete. In many cases, one or two municipalities will upload something that could be interesting if you had access to the same data from all the municipalities, but which is useless as long as only one or two municipalities have uploaded it.

B. Benchmarking using non-citizen-centric indicators

Web sites of Norwegian municipalities are rated every year according to a set of indicators created by DIFI. While the indicator set is tweaked every year, and constantly improving, it still relies heavily on technical indicators, ignoring or downplaying the actual usefulness of the site for citizens. The municipality who was rated top in 2011 is a good example of this. Technically, the site is flawless, but within the Norwegian user experience community it is a running joke, as the site has very poor usability. When one attempts to search or browse for something (for example building permits), you are led through a loop of pages suggesting to click for more information. None of the pages actually contain useful information about what one is looking for; at best, one can find the phone number of someone they can call to get more information. This does not translate only into a waste of citizens' time, but also into lost opportunities for the municipality to get businesses to relocate in the area or new business to start. Even municipalities that are good at publishing content tend to do so following a public sector logic. In order to find documents related to a case, you need to know the case number, the committee(s) that have handled the case etc.

C. Public sector autonomy

Norway has 428 municipalities, all with their own web site. The quality of the web sites varies. The Norwegian Agency for Public Management and eGovernment (DIFI) has done yearly assessments of municipality web sites, awarding grades. The maximum is six stars; the minimum is one star. The yearly assessment shows big differences in the quality. Citizens, at least in the more densely populated areas, often live in one municipality, work in another, shop in a third and attend cultural events in a forth. In practice, the citizen must relate to four web sites with different structure and content.

D. Lack of semantic interoperability

Public administration is not very good at integration across institutional borders. Even if we have had projects addressing semantic interoperability, it will still be years to handle the complexity. This is because words have different semantic meaning in different areas.

While we outline some possible resolutions, none of these barriers are easy to overcome. Technical barriers such as infrastructure, legacy systems and security are very challenging. Creating a common basic infrastructure has been on the agenda in Norway for years, but is still not in place as this is a complex technical issue. The cost of development is also a barrier in some cases. However, these barriers are not impossible to overcome as long as the organizational barriers are addressed first. Public agencies need to collaborate and coordinate their efforts, and involve citizens in the process using the tools of user-centric design.

VIII. Suggestions to Improve Citizen Centricity

The following suggestions are based on our own experience with the development of eGovernment solutions:

A. Build organizational identity

It seems that public organizations are struggling in developing a core organizational identity grounded in both the culture and the traditions from the past and the future aspirations and expectations from both internal and external stakeholders. We suggest a strategy balancing the past and the future – the culture and the image part of organizational identity. The past plays a crucial role in bridging the history, competence and tradition in the past to the future aspirations for public organizations. Hence, the past representing the culture and the future representing the image are connected in a constructive relation in which a citizen-centric public organization may prosper.

B. Involve the citizens

Citizens should be involved at all stages of design, development and assessment of services. The citizens may contribute to better solutions, by providing their needs and wants. Widespread adoption is probably the best measure of success. Citizen involvement may secure the construction of services that will be used by the target group.

C. Share data

Data should be shared with other public sector entities, but it should also include the necessary information about the quality of the data. This will help other public sector entities to assess if data can be used or not. Semantic information should be added to make linking of data easier.

When privacy is not at stake, data can be released as open data sets. This will bring opportunities for third parties to develop new innovative applications that may serve citizens better.

D. Reuse data

Reuse data whenever possible. Citizens should not be required to fill in data that government already possess. With an electronic identity infrastructure, it is possible to connect the citizen to his/her personal profile.

E. Collaborate on web site structure and content

For the citizen, different web site structure and content is a source of confusion. Therefore, efforts should be made to at least provide some common elements on public sector web sites.

F. Spend less time on web site structure

Do not be too concerned about web site structure, but make efforts to make the web sites searchable. Most citizens get frustrated when navigating a complex web site without knowing the structure of the municipality or government entity. Citizens use Google and other search engines. Efforts should be made match the user requests. "I want to build an annex to my house" should be recognized and the citizens should be directed to the relevant web page providing the requested information. This is one reason to work on semantic interoperability.

G. Improve readability

Improve the readability of public sector web sites. Actually, the government has established a program to make content more readable, but still, many government web pages are referring to regulations and rules that can be hard to be understood by most citizens. Make easy-to-understand introductions, and include links to the actual regulations or rules.

H. Protect privacy

Protect the privacy of the citizen. Privacy is important for trust. Privacy statements are common in the private sector. The public sector should explain what the data will be used for, and if it can be shared with other entities. Regulations and procedures should be easily accessible, and appropriate technology should be used to protect the data.

IX. Conclusion and Future Work

In this paper, we have discussed the concept of citizen-centricity in a public sector context. We have shown that being citizen-centric has been an objective for governments for some time, but that in most cases public services are still designed from the point of view of the government entity providing the service, following the logic of government operations and processes. We have discussed how organizational identity can act as a barrier for government becoming truly citizen-centric. We have presented examples from several cases, which show some of the consequences of this failure to be citizen centric. Through the examples of cancer treatment coordinator and user-controlled Pas, we have shown the benefits for society if government is able to become more citizen centric when designing services. Finally, we have presented a set of suggestions that could help government to become citizen centric.

Citizen centricity is not obvious, as shown in several examples in this paper. But there is hope. The examples of cancer coordinators and personal user managed assistants show best practice from the public sector service delivery. The cancer coordinator relieves the patient of the burden of keeping track of all facets of the medical system, and reduces the patient's perception of the complexity of the public sector. The personal user managed assistant provides freedom of choice and empowerment for citizens with impairments. ICT provides great opportunities for creating citizen-centric services. We have provided some suggestions to improve the citizen centricity such services. This paper opens up several new possibilities for research. While we have shown how organizational culture might help explain the lack of citizen-centricity, there is a need for further research in the form of in-depth case studies and action research to uncover exactly how this affects change, and how to change cultures. Further, there is a need for more research, preferably action and/or design-based, in order to create a more comprehensive set of guidelines for citizen-centric government.

ACKNOWLEDGMENT

This work was partially supported by a grant from Iceland, Liechtenstein and Norway, contract type "small size bilateral cooperation projects", "Scholarships and inter-institutional cooperation" program - EEA Financial Mechanism 2009-2014, project number RO15-0059 "Public Sector Renewal Through ICT, A Life-long Learning Approach".

REFERENCES

[1] L. Berntzen, "Citizen-centric eGovernment Services", in *The Sixth International Conference on Advances in Human oriented and Personalized Mechanisms, Technologies, and Services (CENTRIC 2013)*, Venice, Italy, October 27-November 1, pp. 132-136, 2013 [Online]. Available: http://www.thinkmind.org/download_full.php?instance=CENTRIC+2013, [Accessed: June, 2016].

[2] UK Precidency of the European Council, "Ministerial Declaration", Manchester, 2005. Retrieved from: http://www.umic.pt/images/stories/noticias/051124declaration.pdf, [Accessed: June, 2016].

[3] M. Blakemore, N. McDonald, N. Hall, and R. Jucuite, "Delivering citizen-centric public services through technology facilitated organizational change". In *Understanding e-Government in Europe – Issues and Challenges*, P.G. Nixon, V.N. Koutrakou and R. Rawal, Eds. Routledge, 2010, pp. 19-37.

[4] T.A. Undheim and M. Blakemore (Eds.), "A Handbook for Citizen-centric eGovernment", 2007, [Online]. Available: https://joinup.ec.europa.eu/sites/default/files/files_epractice/sites/media/media1781.pdf, [Accessed: June, 2016].

[5] E. Tambouris and K. Tarabanis, "A dialogue-based, life-event oriented, active portal for online one-stop government: The OneStopGov platform", In *dg.o '08 Proceedings of the 2008 International Conference on Digital Government Research*, Digital Government Society of North America, 2008, pp. 405-406.

[6] Portugese Precidency of the European Council, "Ministerial Declaration" Lisbon, 2007. [Online]. Available: http://www.dematerialisedid.com/PDFs/Ministerial_Declaration_Final_Version_120907.pdf, [Accessed: June, 2016].

[7] NET-EUCEN, "What is user-centricity?" (no date) [Online]. Available: http://www.net-eucen.org/usercentric.html, [Accessed: June, 2016].

[8] B. Kaplan and J. Maxwell, "Evaluating the Organizational Impact of Healthcare Information Systems", In *Qualitative Research Methods for Evaluating Computer Information Systems*, J. Anderson and C. Aydin , Eds. Ney York: Springer, 2005, pp. 30-55.

[9] J.W. Cresswell, "Research Design: Qualitative, Quantitative, and Mixed Methods Approach", Sage, Los Angeles, 2009.

[10] A. Ødegård, "Mellom myter, moter, legitimitet og identitet - et studie av norske energiverks læringsroller på reisen fra forvaltning til forretning", Magma, to be published.

[11] S. Albert and D.A. Whetten, "Organizational identity". Res. Organ. Behavior 7, 1985, pp. 263-295.

[12] M.J. Hatch and M. Schultz, "The dynamics of organizational identity", Human Relations, 2002, 55(8), p. 989.

[13] M. Schultz and T. Hernes, "A temporal perspective on organizational identity", Organization Science, 2013, 24(1), pp. 1-21. doi: 10.1287/orsc.1110.0731.

[14] D. Osborne, "Reinventing Government: What a Difference a Strategy Makes", 7th Global Forum on Reinventing Trust in Government. June 26-29, 2009, Vienna, Austria.

[15] E.H. Schein, "Organizational culture and leadership", fourth edition (4th ed ed.), 2010, Jossey-Bass, San Francisco.

[16] Teknisk Ukeblad, "Snart vil alle setene på Flirt-togene være komfortseter", 2014, [Online]. Available: http://www.tu.no/artikler/snart-vil-alle-setene-pa-flirt-togene-vaere-komfortseter/232023, [Accessed: June, 2016].

[17] GOV.UK, "Driving licence counterpart abolished: changes you need to know", 2015, [Online]. Available: https://www.gov.uk/government/news/driving-licence-changes, [Accessed: June, 2016].

[18] D. Travis, "What car park payment machines can teach us about usability", 2014, Userfocus. [Online]. Available: http://www.userfocus.co.uk/articles/car-park-payment-machines.html, [Accessed: June, 2016].

[19] Norwegian Ministry of Health and Care Services, "Together - against cancer", National Cancer Strategy 2013-2017, 2013, [Online]. Available: https://www.regjeringen.no/contentassets/07cd14ff763444a3997de1570b85fad1/i-1158_together-against_cancer_web.pdf, [Accessed: June, 2016].

[20] The Office of the Prime Minister, "Political platform for a government formed by the Conservative Party and the Progress Party", 2013, [Online]. Available: https://www.regjeringen.no/contentassets/a93b067d9b604c5a82bd3b5590096f74/politisk_platform_eng.pdf, [Accessed: June, 2016].

[21] Norwegian Ministry of Health and Care Services, "The Health and Rights Act", 1999, [Online]. Available: https://lovdata.no/dokument/NL/lov/1999-07-02-63#KAPITTEL_2. , [Accessed: June, 2016].

[22] Norwegian Ministry of Local Government and Modernisation, "Digital Agenda for Norway in brief", 2016, [Online]. Available: https://www.regjeringen.no/contentassets/07b212c03fee4d0a94234b101c5b8ef0/en-gb/pdfs/digital_agenda_for_norway_in_brief.pdf, [Accessed: June, 2016].

[23] J. Pfister and G. Schwabe, "Electronic Data Safes as an Infrastructure for Transformational Government? A Case Study". In *Electronic Government: Proceedings of the 14th IFIP WG 8.5 International Conference*, EGOV 2015, Thessaloniki, Greece, August 30 - September 2, 2015, E. Tambouris, M. Janssen, J. H. Scholl, A. M. Wimmer, K. Tarabanis, M. Gascó, B. Klievink, I. Lindgren, and P. Parycek, Eds. Springer International Publishing, 2015, pp. 246-257.

[24] A.F. Van Veenstra, B. Klievink, and M. Janssen, (2011). "Barriers and impediments to transformational government: insights from literature and practice". Electronic Government, An International Journal, 8(2/3), pp. 226–241.

Influence of the Perception of Data Security on Customer Usage of Internet Services

Erik Massarczyk, Peter Winzer
Faculty of Design – Computer Science – Media
RheinMain University of Applied Sciences
Wiesbaden, Germany
Email: erik.massarczyk@hs-rm.de, peter.winzer@hs-rm.de

Abstract—**An increasing customer usage of Internet services with various devices demands a greater effort on data security and privacy issues, because more and more devices are connected and personal data are spread more widely. However, in many cases the performance of services is more important than the provision of data security. So, this leads to a need to investigate how the user perception of data security influences the usage of Internet services, which will be analyzed with the Technology Acceptance Model. Here, the aim of this paper is to figure out a possible negative impact of the perception of data security on the usage of Internet services. The aim of this paper will be that within the usage of the Technology Acceptance Model an influence of data security issues can be proven.**

Keywords-data security; devices; customer usage; Internet services.

I. INTRODUCTION

During the last 10 to 15 years, more and more people use the Internet and Internet services in their daily life. This development leads to a rising global Internet penetration and data flow [1]. Further, most people use mainly services for Social Media, broadcasting/streaming, gaming and cloud computing. Especially during the last years, people start to use the different services with various devices. This approach conducts that people apply more and more different devices for the usage of services [2][3]. Due to this application of services the devices get connected among each other. Hence, it can be assumed, that the personal user data spread to a larger degree [2]. For the customers of Internet services, it is elusive where the personal data is stored and who gets access to the personal data, because the smart connected devices cover wide range of information over geographical boundaries [3][4]. Finally, the usage of Internet services by customers faces the problem of data security and privacy from the user perspective. Personal data include critical information and intellectual properties about the users themselves and these data are countable assets from which enterprises, companies and also criminals can benefit [5].

In general, the users are responsible which personal data they spread for the usage of different Internet services. Hurdle free communication, marketing measures and advertisement disclose also more personal data of the users. Further, a lot of people are also willing to share their personal data in ignorance of risks of data leakage and data theft. Out of it, it can be concluded that data security and privacy gets more and more important, because more personal data is disclosed and often the users are not able to examine who gets access to their personal information and who uses them for legal and illegal motives.

The authors will figure out what the user perception of data security and privacy is, when they use different Internet services with various devices, especially mobile devices with wireless Internet connections. Moreover, each Internet usage is in direct connection with data security and privacy issues. For these reasons, it has to be investigated whether a higher perception of data security and trust in a service leads to a preferred usage of this service or device.

Accordingly, the authors analyze what the users of Internet services do to prevent unauthorized access to their personal data. In Section II, the term data security will be described. Following this section, the authors will figure out the challenges of service and technology usage. In Section IV, the methodology presents the theoretical background of our research and in Section V the further approach will be described.

II. DATA SECURITY

Data security conducts that users want to keep their personal data to themselves. Here, for the user must be clear, who gets access to the personal information. Hence, no one should get access to the user's personal data, who does not have the right permission for the usage [4]. However, a lot of companies use personal data of customers, which customers spread in their Internet services, because a lot of users are not fully aware of the possible risks of sharing information [5][6]. Furthermore, they do not know which huge amount of data they produce and how they can prevent such risks [7]. This behavior could be a problem for residential users, because 56% of Internet services and platforms transmit personal information without permissions to third parties [8]. So, users should be better informed and aware of their personal data. In many cases, persons divulge information, which they may regret in a future situation. Further, the data can be linked to critical personal information like credit card numbers, etc. [5][6].

In general, most users fear: (a) capturing of passwords and accounts, (b) blackmails, (c) eavesdropping, and (d) undesired access to personal data from criminals [2]. The users want a secure transmission of data and the services should guarantee integrity, availability and confidentiality of the data and their transmission [9].

Otherwise, the users also have to prevent unauthorized accesses by changing the passwords regularly, what the authors also investigate with a survey. If the users lose their access and their data is leaked, normally the users have to bear the loss in reputation of image, business partners, relatives and friends [2].

III. CHALLENGES

The main challenge for analyzing user perceptions of data security is that all user attitudes and beliefs are completely subjective and depend on demographic (age) and cultural factors, which influence the customer willing to share data [5]. These discrepancies also include that each user has his perceptions of risks and prevention of risks. As mentioned in Section I, in many cases the people prefer to look for the performance of services instead of the security and data protection measures. To increase the customer caution for disclosure and leakage of private data, services should insert several measures and rules which the customers have to imply to use the services [10]. Further, services and applications should state consequences of misuse and data leakage and insert different messages to make sure that the users understand of their data distribution. However, it is necessary to investigate, what kind of impact the factors have on the individual perception of data security and the influence on the usage of Internet services, especially mobile services.

IV. METHODOLOGY

For the analysis of the connection between the perception of data security and the usage of Internet services, the authors will use the Technology Acceptance Model (TAM). The TAM shall clarify, how the customer individual's acceptance of Information Technologies (IT) can be explained and predicted [11][12]. Our paper will focus on the dependence of the usage of mobile Internet services on security issues and the acceptance of new technologies. It is currently known that the perceived usefulness has a positive impact on behavioral intentions, which turns in an actual customer usage [12]. However, perceived usefulness does not cover the user's perception, that the usage of the service will enhance his performance [11].

Moreover, perceived usefulness and behavioral intentions are not able to analyze and to reflect user perceptions of data security and the adoption of mobile Internet services. Therefore, the authors implement an external variable as influence factor for perceived usefulness. The external variable will be perceived credibility, which covers the user beliefs and attitudes that the used systems would be free of privacy and security threats [13]. Lin et al. further figured out that data security and privacy are the most affecting factors for an adoption of technology [13]. It is also known that perceived credibility influence positively the behavioral intention to use [14]. But, the authors do not conclude that users believe that using mobile Internet services will not imply security or privacy threats [14]. Here, the authors are of the opinion that the customers carry security and privacy threats by using mobile Internet services. To examine this hypothesis, the authors will use a survey to prove that data security issues have a negative impact on behavioral intentions to use mobile Internet services. For the analysis of the individual customer groups, separate cross-sectional surveys ("one-shot survey") will be conducted within a short period of time [15]. Here, the answers are taken by interviewers in personal oral interviews, thus ensuring completeness and accuracy of the answers. The personal interview will be conducted on the basis of a random quota sample based on the demographic characteristics of gender and age in order to be representative of the local population [16][17]. To cover the frequency of mobile data usage and the perception of data security, a 5-point-Likert-scale (very often to very few and very important to very important) will be implemented. The discrepancy to the previous study will be underlined by the analysis of other impact factors like culture values and traditions.

V. APPROACH

The idea of this paper is to present a relationship between a perception of data security and usage of Internet services, especially of mobile Internet services. After a review of literature to gain an overview about existing concepts and theories over customer behaviors in circumstances of data security issues, a survey shall find out and investigate current customer Internet behaviors. The data will be analyzed with quantitative research methods under usage of the statistical program Statistical Package for the Social Sciences (SPSS). After the evaluation credibility, the Exploratory Factor Analysis will be done to ensure the validity and to present related groups of perceptions and services. The analysis of the survey shall present the regression between the external variable perceived credibility and perceived usefulness and behavioral intentions. After completion of the data analysis, next steps aim at figuring out the results of least square regression and completion to support the hypothesis and findings of the TAM in relation of data security issues.

REFERENCES

[1] International Telecommunication Union (ITU), "ICT Facts & Figures – The world in 2015", May 2015, [Online]. https://www.itu.int/en/ITU-D/Statistics/Documents/facts/ICTFactsFigures2015.pdf, 2016.07.11.

[2] P. W. Dowd and J. T. McHenry, "Network Security: It's Time to Take It Seriously" Computer (1998), vol. 31, issue 9, IEEE, Sept. 1998, pp. 24-28.

[3] D. Desai, "Law and Technology – Beyond Location: Data Security in the 21st Century" Magazine Communications of the ACM (2013), vol. 56, issue 1, ACM, Jan. 2013, pp. 34-36.

[4] F. S. Ferraz and C. A. Guimarães Ferraz, "Smart City Security Issues: Depicting information security issues in the role of a urban environment", 7th International Conference on

Utility and Cloud Computing, IEEE/ACM, 2014, pp. 842-846.

[5] S. Dhawan, K. Singh, and S. Goel, "Impact of Privacy Attitude. Concern and Awareness on Use of Online Social Networking" 5th International Conference - Confluence The Next Generation Information Technology Summit 2013, IEEE, Sept. 2014, pp. 14-17.

[6] D. Malandrino, V. Scarano, and R. Spinelli, "How increased awareness can impact attitudes and behaviors toward online privacy protection", International Conference on Social Computing (Social Com), IEEE, Sept. 2013, pp. 57-62.

[7] A. N. Joinson. U.-D. Reips, T. Buchanan, and C. B. Paine Schofield, "Privacy, Trust, and Self-Disclosure Online", Human-Computer Interaction, vol. 25, no. 1, 2010, pp. 1-24.

[8] B. Krishnamurthy, K. Naryshkin, and C. Wills, "Privacy leakage vs. protection measures: the growing disconnect", in Web 2.0 Security and Privacy Workshop, 2011, pp. 1-10.

[9] D. Nayak, N. Rajendran, D. B. Phatak, and V. P. Gulati, "Security Issues in Mobile Data Networks" Vehicular Technology Conference (VTC 2004), vol. 5, IEEE , Sept. 2004, pp. 3229-3233.

[10] Q. Tan and F. Pivot, "Big Data Privacy: Changing Perception of Privacy, International Conference on Smart City/SocialCom/SustainCom, IEEE, 2015, pp. 860-865

[11] F. D. Davis, "Perceived usefulness, perceived ease of use, and user acceptance of information technology", MIS Quarterly, Vol. 13, 1989, pp. 318-340.

[12] F. D. Davis, R. P. Bagozzi, and P. R. Warshaw, "User acceptance of computer technology: a comparison of two theoretical models", Management Science, Vol. 35, 1989, pp. 982-1003.

[13] F.-T. Lin, H.-Y. Wu, and T. T. Nguyet Nga, "Adoption of Internet Banking: An Empirical Study in Vietnam", 10th International Conference on e-Business Engnineering, IEEE, 2013, pp. 282-287.

[14] Y. S. Wang, Y. M. Wang, H. H. Lin, and T. I. Tang, "Determinants of user acceptance of Internet banking: an empirical study", International Journal of Service Industry Management, vol. 14, 2003, pp. 501-519.

[15] A. Diekmann, „Empirical Social Research", [German] „Empirische Sozialforschung", Reinbek / Hamburg, Rowohlt-Taschenbuch-Verlag, Vol. 5, 2011

[16] J. Bortz and N. Döring, „Research Methods and Evaluations", [German] „Forschungsmethoden und Evaluation; für Human- und Sozialwissenschaftler", Heidelberg, Springer-Medizin-Verlag, vol. 4, 2009

[17] M. Kaya, „Data Collection Procedure", [German] „Verfahren der Datenerhebung", in Albers, S./Klapper, D./Konradt, U./Walter, A./Wolf, J. (Hrsg.): *Methodik der empirischen Forschung*, Wiesbaden, Gabler, vol. 3, 2013, pp. 49-64.

Improving Special Purpose Machine User-Interfaces by Machine-Learning Algorithms

Valentin Plenk

Institute of Information Systems
Hof University of Applied Sciences
95028 Hof, Germany
Email: valentin.plenk@iisys.de

***Abstract*—This paper proposes to make complex production machines more user-friendly. Improved machines help the operator in case of an error message or a process event by displaying recommendations, such as "in the last 10 occurences of this event the operators performed the following keystrokes". The messages are generated from statistical data on former user-interaction and previous process-events. The data represents the knowledge of all the machine operators. The data is gathered by logging user-interaction and process-events during regular operation of the production machine. This approach allows to store the operators' expert knowledge in the production machine without human intervention.**

Keywords–machine-learning; human machine interfaces; special-purpose machines; production machines

I. Introduction

State of the art appliances (e.g., photocopiers) are equipped with user interfaces that help the operator fix problems (e.g., a paper jam). The implementation of the software driving the interface contains structured knowledge about error scenarios and step by step instructions on how to deal with them.

While this approach leads to very well usable appliances, its proliferation is hampered by the engineering effort required for the definition of the error scenarios. This effort is only economically reasonable, if it can be refinanced over a large number of appliances. In the context of production machines, particularily special purpose machines, where the usual lot size is in a range below 10 similar machines per annum [1], a different approach is needed.

To deal with that problem, the author proposes to use machine-learning algorithms to generate situation-specific user guidance information from former user interactions and previous process events. Figure 6 shows a screenshot of the prototype displaying recommendations for fixing an error.

Similar applications of machine learning algorithms are commonly used to enhance user interfaces in smartphones or other IT-systems [2], [3]. In the production-machine sector, however, the application of machine learning algorithms is apparently limited to applications dealing with pattern detection in process data or distingushing different datasets [4]–[7]. In these papers the authors use the output of the algorithms to detect errors or problems with production quality. This information is then presented to the production-machine operator, requesting him to deal with the situation. While this approach undoubtedly helps to make processes more stable, it also demands ever more expertise of the operators.

In Section II, we describe how we model the production-process to make machine-learning applicable and give an overview of the system structure and the test environment. In Section III, we detail how we generate the events for the model and present the mechanisms generating the recommendations. In Section IV we evaluate the recommendations generated by our algorithm. Section V briefly summarizes our findings so far and then gives an outlook on our work plan for the future.

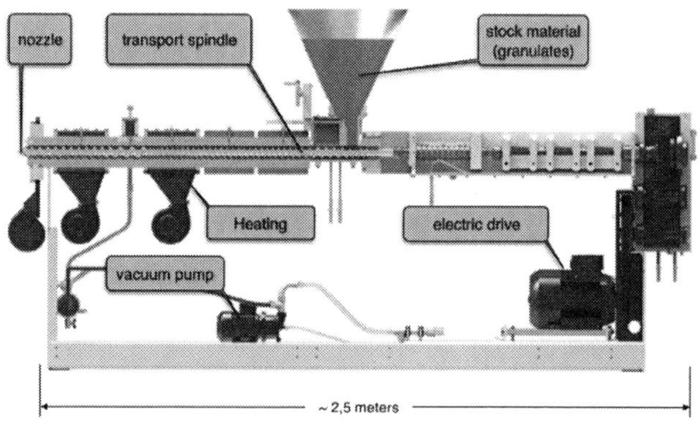

Figure 1. Working principle of an extruder
(courtesy: Hans Weber Maschinenfabrik, Kronach, Germany)

II. Proposed Approach and Test Environment

Machine-learning algorithms work on event sequences. Therefore we need to model the production process as a sequence of events. Such an event represents one out of a limited number of conditions and the time when the condition became true. Some events are generated by the process, i.e., error messages, and some events are generated by the operator, i.e., commands.

By logging these events over a significant amount of time, we can build a map of event sequences and their frequency.

Once the production machine encounters an error condition and prompts the operator for interaction, we use this map to find user interactions that were made in prior occurrences of the error condition and display a list of these interactions as recommended actions (Figure 6).

We develop the system on a simulated production machine. The machine in question is a plastics extruder (see Figure 1). The basic purpose of this machine is to transport and melt plastic granulates by means of a threaded spindle towards a nozzle. The main process parameters are the speed of the spindle, the temperature of the extruded material and the pressure of the material at the nozzle.

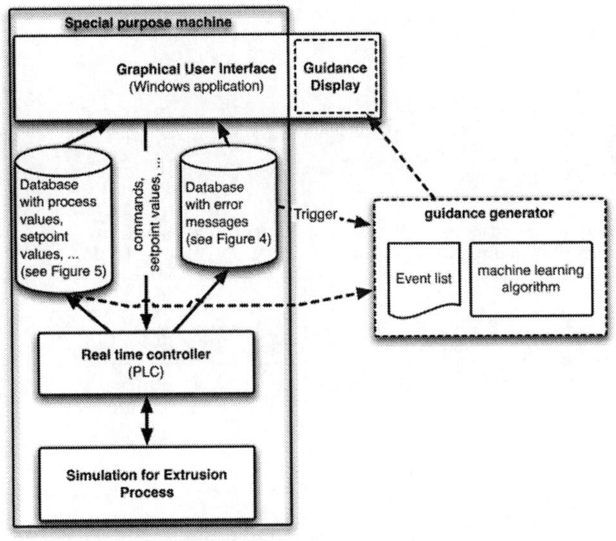

Figure 2. Structure of the system
(solid lines: standard control system; dotted lines: additions for recommendation mechanism)

Figure 2 shows the structure of the machine control system. The user interface is running on windows and communicates with the real time controller, a PLC, via two databases.

One database contains a log of all error-messages (Figure 4).

The other database contains a log of all PLC variables (Figure 5). Each row holds the values of all the variables at a given time. Each column corresponds to a PLC variable. There are variables representing process values, e.g., temperature values (`Loop1_PV`) or the pressure at the nozzle (`MP1_Value`), and variables representing parameters entered by the operator, e.g., temperature setpoints (`Loop1_SP`). The actual database has approximately 100 columns.

For our development, the actual control system is coupled to a simulation model of the extruder. An operator is running the simulated machine, thereby generating and fixing errors.

III. Generation of Events and User Guidance

Figure 2 shows that we added a guidance generator. The generator is a separate application running in parallel to the graphical user interface. This application is polling the database with the PLC variables shown in Figure 5 and processes it into an event list.

This processing is based on a description of the columns: which columns contain parameters and which columns contain process values.

For parameter columns the algorithm compares two consecutive rows and generates an event for each column that differs. These events represent operator interactions. They are coded as string values, e.g., `Loop2_SP_170`, containing the name of the PLC variable and the value of the new setpoint.

For process variables we use a different approach to represent the continuously variable values: First we calculate the deviation from the setpoint of the variable

$$Var_{rel} = \left| \frac{Var_{Process}}{Var_{Setpoint}} \cdot 100\% \right|$$

Then we sort Var_{rel} into one of the classes shown in Table I and generate an event every time the process value enters a new class. These events are also coded as string values, e.g., `Loop_1_2_PV_X`.

TABLE I. CLASSES FOR PROCESS VARIABLES

Var_{rel}	$\leq 1.77\%$	$\leq 3.16\%$	$\leq 5.62\%$	$\leq 10.0\%$	$\leq 17.78\%$
Class	A	B	C	D	E
Var_{rel}	$\leq 31.62\%$	$\leq 56.23\%$	$\leq 100.0\%$	$\leq 177.8\%$	$> 177.8\%$
Class	F	G	H	I	X

When the machine needs operator assistance, i.e., it has added a new row with an error message in the error message database (Figure 4), our guidance generation algorithm is triggered.

The algorithm then scans all past events in the event list to generate an event sequence map of both process variables and operator interactions that has led to the current error message. The length of the generated event sequences has to be limited. For now, we use all events that occurred in the five minutes before the error message.

The event sequences are stored in a content addressable memory, i.e., a Java map, where the events before the error message are used as the key, whereas the value represents a list of all operator interaction events between the time the error condition became true and the time the error condition became false again. For each of these sequences, the map also contains the frequency of the respective sequence in the past.

Figure 3 shows an abbreviated example for the map. The key `Loop1_2_SP_0# Loop1_3_SP_0# Loop_1_2_PV_X# Loop1_3_PV_X#1101` consists of a concatenated sequence of process variable, operator interaction and error events. The value `Loop1_2_SP_170#Loop1_3_SP_170# ==> 3` consists of a concatenation of operator interaction events and their frequency in the past.

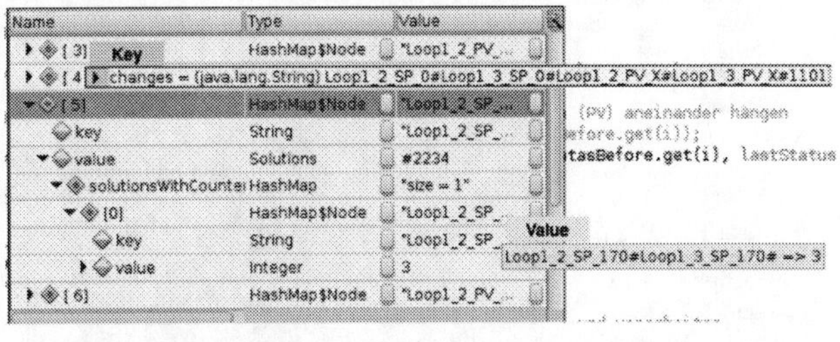

Figure 3. One entry in the event-sequence map of the guidance generation algorithm

The three most frequent interaction event sequences are stored in the error database. Once the operator requests guidance by selecting an error message in the error list on the right of the user interface, shown in Figure 6, the modified user interface of the machine reads this field, decodes the coded string and displays the guidance box shown on the left of Figure 6.

	Start	Acknowledge	End	Removed	AlarmNumber	TextSchnipsel	ID	Recommendation
1	2016-06-30 14:46:04	[NULL]	2016-06-30 14:51:09	[NULL]	22	[NULL]	852	[NULL]
2	2016-06-30 14:46:02	[NULL]	2016-06-30 14:53:54	[NULL]	1.002	[NULL]	851	[NULL]
3	2016-06-30 14:46:01	[NULL]	2016-06-30 14:53:54	[NULL]	12	[NULL]	850	[NULL]
4	2016-06-30 14:43:23	[NULL]	2016-06-30 14:43:38	[NULL]	2.006	2016-06-30_14-43-21.jpg	849	[NULL]
5	2016-06-30 14:43:11	[NULL]	2016-06-30 14:43:26	[NULL]	2.006	2016-06-30_14-43-02.jpg	848	[NULL]
6	2016-06-30 14:37:39	[NULL]	2016-06-30 14:46:41	[NULL]	1.101	[NULL]	847	3#Loop1_2@1@170#Loop1_3@1@170
7	2016-06-30 14:19:31	[NULL]	2016-06-30 14:46:41	[NULL]	2.221	[NULL]	846	[NULL]
8	2016-06-30 14:19:31	[NULL]	2016-06-30 14:46:41	[NULL]	2.211	[NULL]	845	[NULL]

Figure 4. Part of the error message database
(line 6 shows the error and the recommendation displayed in Figure 6)

	ID	TimeStamp	Loop1_2_SP	Loop1_2_PV	Loop1_3_SP	Loop1_3_PV	MP1_Value
1	629.027	2016-06-30 14:33:47	170	170	170	170	98
2	629.029	2016-06-30 14:34:07	0	169,8	0	170	98
3	629.031	2016-06-30 14:34:27	0	162,7	0	166,8	98,1
4	629.033	2016-06-30 14:34:47	0	152,4	0	162	98,4
5	629.035	2016-06-30 14:35:07	0	142,2	0	157	98,6
6	629.037	2016-06-30 14:35:27	0	132,7	0	152,1	98,8
7	629.039	2016-06-30 14:35:47	0	124	0	147,5	99
8	629.041	2016-06-30 14:36:07	0	115,9	0	143	99,2
9	629.043	2016-06-30 14:36:28	0	108,5	0	138,8	99,4
10	629.045	2016-06-30 14:36:48	0	101,7	0	134,7	99,6
11	629.047	2016-06-30 14:37:08	0	95,5	0	130,8	99,8
12	629.049	2016-06-30 14:37:28	0	89,7	0	127,1	99,9
13	629.051	2016-06-30 14:37:48	0	84,4	0	123,5	100
14	629.053	2016-06-30 14:38:08	0	79,6	0	120,1	100,2

Figure 5. Part of the PLC variable database
(the error shown in Figure 4 occurs in line 13)

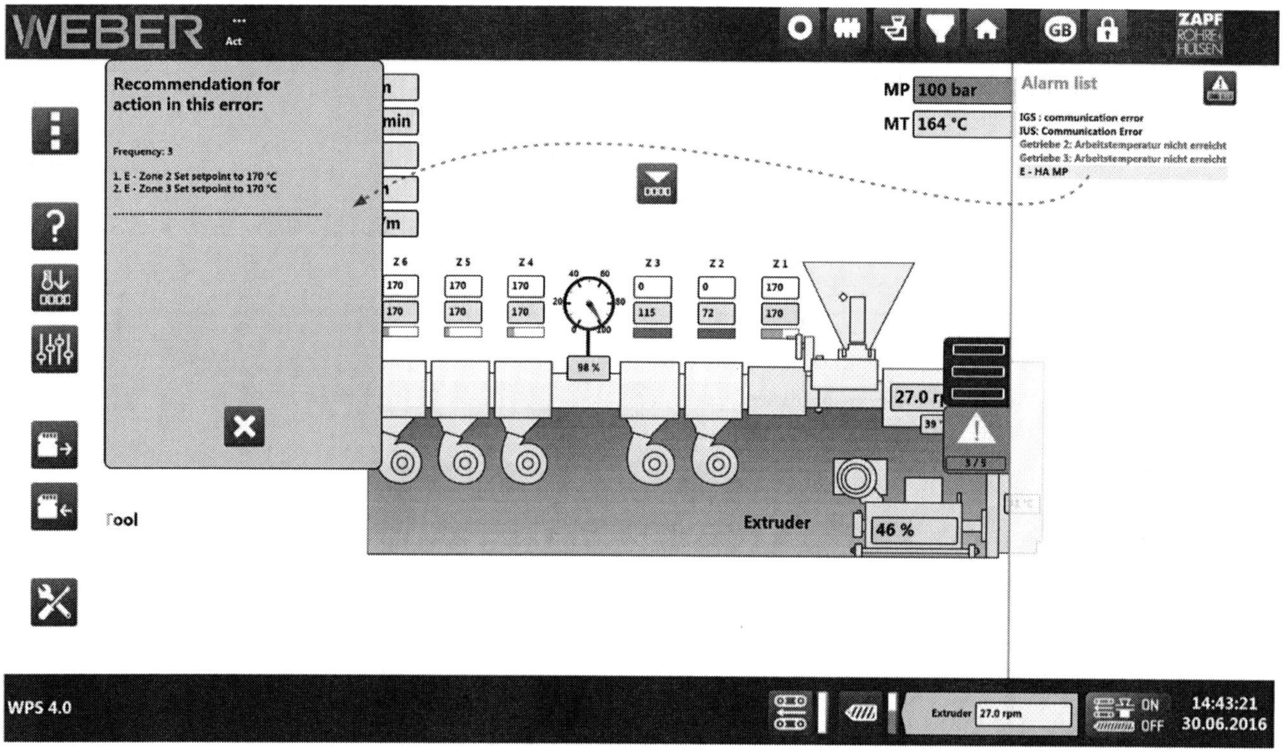

Figure 6. An example user guidance screen
(list of error messages on the right side; selection of last error message in list displays recommendation for action on the left side)

IV. Quality of Recommendations

We simulated production and user interaction on the actual user interface and PLC connected to the simulation model. The resulting PLC variable database partly shown in Figure 5 now contains 713.677 rows with approximately 100 process values. The error message database partly shown in Figure 4 contains 1050 error messages. 163 of these messages were caused by the error event `1101`. During our operation of the simulated machine we cleared 140 of these error events by performing operations via the user interface. We cleared the remaining error events by resetting the simulation model.

In these 163 occurrences our algorithm identified 40 different event-sequences that led to the error event `1101`. Table III shows a part of that event-sequence map. The key is shown at the top of the row, sometimes spanning multiple lines. The number to the left of the lines following the key represents the number of cases (frequency) in which the user performed the operation sequence shown in that line (value). In many cases the operation-sequences in the map are identical, but tied to different event-sequences.

Table II shows the 9 different operation sequences from Table III. These operation sequences were derived solely from logged process data.

TABLE II. OPERATION SEQUENCES FROM THE EVENT SEQUENCE MAP SHOWN IN TABLE III

Operation sequence	Frequency
`AOut1_1_27#`	93
`Loop1_2_SP_170# Loop1_3_SP_170#`	38
`Loop1_2_SP_170# Loop1_3_SP_170# Loop1_4_SP_170#`	3
`AOut1_1_27# AOut1_1_28# AOut1_1_27#`	2
`Loop1_2_SP_250# Loop1_3_SP_250#`	2
`AOut1_1_29#`	1
`AOut1_2_2# AOut1_2_3# AOut1_2_5# AOut1_2_7# AOut1_2_8# AOut1_2_9#`	1
`Loop1_2_SP_200# Loop1_3_SP_200# Loop1_2_SP_250# Loop1_3_SP_250#`	1
`Loop1_3_SP_170# Loop1_4_SP_170#`	1

On that basis, we can provide the operator with different recommendations for clearing the error event `1101`. This is significantly better than tying a predefined help message to the error.

Table II also shows that some operation sequences were performed much more frequently than others. The first two sequences cover 93 % of all occurences of the error event.

V. Conclusion and Future Work

One important result of our work so far is a structure for interfacing a special-purpose machine with a guidance generation mechanism. The interface requirements are fairly easy to meet: (a) there must be a way to read all (relevant) PLC-variables, (b) for each variable, we need to know whether it represents a process variable or a process parameter, and (c) we need a way to trigger the guidance generation. This allows for a wide range of machines to be interfaced.

The way we convert changing process values and changed process parameters into discrete events allows us to apply machine-learning algorithms to the problem.

Our first, quite simple approach, loosely based on Markov-Chains, already shows a promising potential: We can generate recommendations solely from logged process data. These findings justify deeper research. We have therefore applied for funding to continue our work.

For the near future, we plan to collect real data from customers using the production machines in their companies. We plan to equip these production machines with a "black box" that contains the guidance generator and interfaces with the machines. The display of the hints can either be done on the machine user interface or on a separate user interface in the "black box".

Once we have collected a sufficient number of interactions, we will test a variety of machine learning algorithms. We see two issues with the application of the algorithms:

First: We use the event sequence before the trigger as a search criterion. Which / how many events should be included in the search key?

Second: Because of the slow response time of the process / the machine there can be delays in the order of magnitude of several minutes between a user interaction and a significant change in the process. This makes it possible that some user interaction events occur between the time an error condition has become true and false again (after user intervention). In that case, it will be difficult to distinguish between "helpful" and "intermediate / time filling" interactions. Which events should be included in the recommendation?

Current user feedback shows that it will also be necessary to structure the results of the learning algorithms in a way that allows a proficient user to specifiy "nonsensical" interactions and to remove them from the knowledge base. This requirement might be hard to meet, since statistics based learning algorithms do not provide a way to tie outputs to one of the many input sets.

As a long-term goal, we think about generating our own trigger events by changing the way we search the event database. By comparing the current event sequence to event sequences stored before an error event, we can recommend an interaction before the event occurs that triggered it in the past. By coupling that approach with a function in the "black box" allowing the operator to indicate why he interacted with the machine, the operator can mark event sequences that require intervention. On the basis of these marked sequences, we can then recommend interactions for problems that the original machine software cannot detect.

References

[1] V. Plenk, "A benchmark for embedded software processes used by special-purpose machine manufacturers," in Proceedings of the third international Conference on Software Engineering Advances. Los Alamonitos: CPS, 2008, pp. 166 – 171.

[2] H. J. C. et al., "Learning styles diagnosis based on user interface behaviors for the customization of learning interfaces in an intelligent tutoring system," in Proceedings of the 8th International Conference on Intelligent Tutoring Systems (ITS 2006). Jhongli, Taiwan: Springer, June 26-30 2006, pp. 513 – 524.

[3] B. D. Davison and H. Hirsh, "Predicting sequences of user actions," in AAAI Technical Report WS-98-07, 1998, pp. 5 – 12.

[4] P. K. Wonga, J. Zhonga, Z. Yanga, and C. M. Vong, "Sparse bayesian extreme learning committee machine for engine simultaneous fault diagnosis," in Neurocomputing, 2016, pp. 331 – 343.

[5] K. Zidek, A. Hosovsky, and J. Dubjak, "Diagnostics of surface errors by embedded vision system and its classification by machine learning algorithms," in Key Engineering Materials, 2015, pp. 459 – 466.

[6] J. Luo, C.-M. Vong, and P.-K. Wong, "Sparse bayesian extreme learning machine for multi-classification," in IIEEE Transactions on Neural Networks and Learning Systems, 2014, pp. 836 – 843.

[7] A. Ziaja, I. Antoniadou, T. Barszcz, W. J. Staszewski, and K. Worden, "Fault detection in rolling element bearings using wavelet-based variance analysis and novelty detection," Journal of Vibration and Control, vol. 22, no. 2, February 2016, pp. 396–411.

[8] J. Lunze, Ereignisdiskrete Systeme. München: Oldenbourg, 2006.

TABLE III. PART OF THE EVENT-SEQUENCE MAP FOR ERROR 1101
(To save space, we do not show all of the less frequent keys.)

Key	Freq.	Value
AOut1_1_27# MP1_99# AIn1_1_27# AIn1_2_46# AIn2_1_539# AOut1_1_28# MP1_103# AIn1_1_28# AIn1_2_47# AIn2_1_560# 1101		
	4	AOut1_1_27#
AIn1_2_46# MP1_100# MP1_101# 1101		
	3	Loop1_2_SP_170# Loop1_3_SP_170#
AOut1_1_28# MP1_101# AIn1_1_28# AIn1_2_46# AIn2_1_56# 1101		
	4	AOut1_1_27#
	1	Loop1_2_SP_250# Loop1_3_SP_250#
Loop1_2_SP_0# Loop1_3_SP_0# Loop1_2_PV_X# Loop1_3_PV_X# MP1_99# AIn1_2_46# MP1_100# 1101		
	23	Loop1_2_SP_170# Loop1_3_SP_170#
Loop1_2_SP_0# Loop1_3_SP_0# Loop1_2_PV_X# Loop1_3_PV_X# MP1_100# MP1_101# 1101		
	2	Loop1_2_SP_170# Loop1_3_SP_170#
AOut1_1_28# MP1_103# AIn1_1_28# AIn1_2_47# AIn2_1_560# 1101		
	66	AOut1_1_27#
	1	AOut1_1_29#
	1	AOut1_1_27# AOut1_1_28# AOut1_1_27#
MP1_100# AIn2_1_544# AOut1_1_28# MP1_103# AIn1_1_28# AIn1_2_47# AIn2_1_560# 1101		
	1	AOut1_1_27#
Loop1_2_SP_0# Loop1_2_PV_X# Loop1_3_SP_0# Loop1_3_PV_X# MP1_99# AIn1_2_46# MP1_100# 1101		
	2	Loop1_2_SP_170# Loop1_3_SP_170#
MP1_100# Loop1_2_PV_B# Loop1_2_PV_C# Loop1_3_PV_A# Loop1_2_SP_0# Loop1_3_SP_0# Loop1_2_PV_X# Loop1_3_PV_X# MP1_101# 1101		
	1	Loop1_2_SP_170# Loop1_3_SP_170#
Loop1_2_PV_A# MP1_100# Loop1_2_PV_B# Loop1_3_PV_A# Loop1_2_PV_C# Loop1_3_PV_B# Loop1_2_PV_D# Loop1_4_PV_A# Loop1_3_PV_C# Loop1_4_PV_B# Loop1_2_PV_E# Loop1_2_SP_0# Loop1_3_SP_0# Loop1_4_SP_0# Loop1_2_PV_X# Loop1_3_PV_X# Loop1_4_PV_X# MP1_101# 1101		
	1	Loop1_2_SP_170# Loop1_3_SP_170# Loop1_4_SP_170#
AIn2_1_555# AOut1_1_28# MP1_101# AIn1_1_28# AIn1_2_46# AIn2_1_560# AOut1_1_27# MP1_99# AIn1_1_27# AIn1_2_45# AIn2_1_539# MP1_98# AOut1_1_28# MP1_101# AIn1_1_28# AIn1_2_46# AIn2_1_560# 1101		
	1	AOut1_1_27#
Loop1_2_PV_A# MP1_100# Loop1_2_PV_B# Loop1_3_PV_A# Loop1_2_SP_0# Loop1_3_SP_0# Loop1_2_PV_X# Loop1_3_PV_X# MP1_101# 1101		
	1	Loop1_2_SP_170# Loop1_3_SP_170#
AIn1_4_97# AOut1_1_8# MP1_29# AIn1_1_8# AIn1_2_13# AIn2_1_16# AOut1_1_16# MP1_63# AIn1_1_16# AIn1_2_29# AIn2_1_32# AOut1_1_24# MP1_96# AIn1_1_24# AIn1_2_44# AIn2_1_49# AOut1_1_27# MP1_109# AIn1_1_27# AIn1_2_50# AIn2_1_53# 1101		
	1	AOut1_2_2# AOut1_2_3# AOut1_2_5# AOut1_2_7# AOut1_2_8# AOut1_2_9#
Loop1_2_PV_A# AIn2_1_555# AOut1_1_28# MP1_101# AIn1_1_28# AIn1_2_46# AIn2_1_560# 1101		
	1	AOut1_1_27# AOut1_1_28# AOut1_1_27#
AOut1_1_28# MP1_102# AIn1_1_28# AIn1_2_47# AIn2_1_560# MP1_103# 1101		
	4	AOut1_1_27#
AOut1_1_28# MP1_101# AIn1_1_28# AIn1_2_46# AIn2_1_560# 1101		
	1	Loop1_2_SP_250# Loop1_3_SP_250#
	1	Loop1_2_SP_200# Loop1_3_SP_200# Loop1_2_SP_250# Loop1_3_SP_250#
AOut1_1_28# MP1_103# AIn1_1_28# AIn1_2_47# AIn2_1_560# AOut1_1_27# MP1_99# AIn1_1_27# AIn1_2_46# AIn2_1_539# AOut1_1_28# MP1_103# AIn1_1_28# AIn1_2_47# AIn2_1_560# 1101		
	1	AOut1_1_27#
MP1_100# AIn2_1_541# AOut1_1_28# MP1_103# AIn1_1_28# AIn1_2_47# AIn2_1_560# 1101		
	2	AOut1_1_27#
AOut1_1_27# MP1_100# AIn1_1_27# AIn1_2_46# AIn2_1_539# MP1_99# AOut1_1_28# MP1_103# AIn1_1_28# AIn1_2_47# AIn2_1_560# 1101		
	2	AOut1_1_27#
MP1_100# Loop1_2_PV_B# Loop1_2_PV_C# Loop1_3_PV_A# Loop1_3_PV_B# Loop1_2_PV_D# Loop1_3_PV_C# Loop1_2_PV_E# Loop1_2_SP_0# Loop1_3_SP_0# Loop1_2_PV_X# Loop1_3_PV_X# MP1_101# 1101		
	1	Loop1_2_SP_170# Loop1_3_SP_170#
AOut1_1_28# MP1_102# AIn1_1_28# AIn1_2_47# AIn2_1_560# 1101		
	1	AOut1_1_27#
Loop1_2_SP_60# Loop1_3_SP_60# Loop1_2_PV_I# Loop1_3_PV_I# Loop1_2_PV_H# Loop1_3_PV_H# MP1_99# AIn1_2_46# Loop1_2_PV_G# Loop1_3_PV_G# MP1_100# 1101		
	1	Loop1_2_SP_170# Loop1_3_SP_170#

Keyboard Input by Movement of the Finger and Pointer using a Smart Device

[1]Jungpil Shin, [1]Hiromasa Omote, [2]Cheol Min Kim

[1]School of Computer Science and Engineering,
The University of Aizu, Fukushima, Japan
E-mail: jpshin@u-aizu.ac.jp
[2]Department of Computer Education, Jeju National University, Korea
E-mail: cmkim@jejunu.ac.kr

***Abstract*— Nowadays, users of smartphones use keyboard input, flick input and multi-tap input. Moreover, there are keyboard input and handwritten character input using a pen tablet for the PC. There is some input methods based on handwriting of characters in the air using Kinect and a web camera in much research. However, character input by using devices such as Kinect and a web camera are limited by the environment. The user also needs to learn a new input method because many systems use the original character input method. We reduce the burden of users by using a smart device with a high penetration rate. Moreover, we use the keyboard input method because it is a general input method. Therefore, users do not need to learn a new input method. Our method can be used by the various environments by using a smart device. Since character input from long distance can be performed using a camera of a smart device moreover, our method can be used broadly.**

Keywords- Keyboard Input; Finger Recognition; Smart Device

I. INTRODUCTION

In recent years, the number of character input methods has increased significantly. For example, there is keyboard input, voice input and handwriting input on the PC. Table 1 shows the research about character input method. There is handwritten input in the air using Kinect [1] and character input using Leap Motion [2]. Moreover, there is smartphone and tablet keyboard input, multi-tap input, flick input and the voice input.

However, users need to learn the newly developed character input method. It is a burden for users.

Currently, there are many devices using character input. For example, there is the keyboard, web camera, Kinect, Leap Motion, the pen tablet and the microphone. These devices are used as accessory devices on a PC. Therefore, users are limited to a location to use the device.

Smart devices are evolving. Therefore, smart devices will be larger in size. Moreover, the spread of smart phones increases character input in the usage of the Internet. However, the conventional character input system cannot correspond to the difference among the possessors and the length of a user's finger. Therefore, the character input of a smart device does not have good operability.

There are a lot of recognition methods for the finger and the hand. Some examples are the hand recognition using a depth camera [10], Kinect recognition of the hand and fingertip [11] and recognition using a colour glove [12]. However, these methods require a special tool. Therefore, users cannot easily use these systems. Special tools do not have a high penetration rate. So, users do not use the recognition system.

We solve this problem by using a smart device. This paper has three purposes. First, users can input characters regardless of the location and the environment. This system uses only a smart device, so this system does not require a special tool. Therefore, users are not limited to a location and environment to use this system. Second, users can input characters without special tools. Last, users can input characters at a remote location. Users can input characters without touching the screen by using this system. Therefore, users can input characters at a remote location. Users can input by touching using the virtual keyboard that is displayed on the screen of the smart device by the camera. The method of inputting characters uses the keyboard input that is most used in the PC and smart device. Users do not need to learn a new character input method by using the keyboard input method. An accessory device of a PC is used in most study about character input. This system is an input of the character using the front camera of a smart device. Therefore, users can easily use this system because this system does not need an attached device.

This system recognizes fingertips by using hue recognition and template matching. Hue recognition gets the hue information of users in advance. Thereby, this

TABLE I. RELATED PAPERSR OF THE CHARACTER INPUT METHOD

Researchers	Using Device	Main Device	Method of a Character Input
M. Fujimoto et al. [3]	Original Device	PC	Keyboard
N. Matsui et al. [4]	RGB-Camera	PC	Original Keyboard
M. Weiss et al. [5]	SLAP	PC	Virtual Keyboard
Y. Nishida et al. [6]	Kinect	PC	Aerial Handwritten
M. Kaneko et al. [7]	Non	Smart Device	Original Method
S. Takahiro et al. [8]	Non	Smart Device	Original Method
R. Yamamoto et al. [9]	Earphone	Smart Device	None

system correctly recognizes the background and fingertips. In addition, only the hue recognition recognizes the fingertips. Therefore, this system is template matching using a fingertip image of users.

This system is available (1) in the any impossible place to touch such as surgery, (2) any environment without PC or Camera and (3) any remote place in the range of appropriate distance.

In Section 2 we show the approaches for keyboard input. In Section 3 we show the experiment and results. In Section 4 we show the discussions. In Section 5 we conclude the paper.

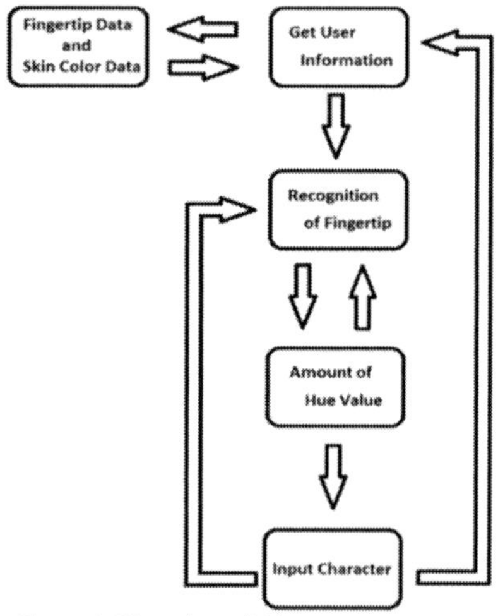

Figure 1. Flow chart of this system

II. Keyboard Input Approaches

This system targets a device, such as a smart phone, to operate it by touching the screen. This system uses a front camera of a device. So, users do not need to have a new device.

This system performs the character input by the step shown in Fig. 1. First, this system gets the information of the user's hand. It is the colour information of the skin and fingertip information. The colour of the skin and the shape of the hand of each person are different. We increase the accuracy of this system by corresponding it to the difference of shapes and colours. In addition, input is done by fingertip's touching the virtual keyboard using the camera. Therefore, we need the recognition with high accuracy. We explain these steps in detail.

A. System Simulation

This system gets the information of a user's hand before the character input. First, the screen of the device is projected as in Fig. 2. Users see their fingertip on the green square. Then, the user presses a button on the bottom centre of the screen. As a result, the screen changes to the character input screen. As shown in Fig. 3, on the character input screen, a virtual keyboard and a red square are projected. The user moves the fingertip to the position of the character. Then, the fingertip selects the virtual keyboard character by contact. This system can also recognize objects that are not a fingertip. However, this research is mainly performed on the use of fingertip.

B. Get User Data, Skin-color data and Fingertip data

This system gets the information of the user's hand before the character input. The user information is necessary to get correctly because it changes the accuracy of the character input system. The user's information for recognition is the colour of skin and information on a fingertip. The colour of the skin is different in a person respectively. It is the cause of recognition errors. In addition, the colour of the skin changes by a change in the environment like the brightness. Therefore, we increase the accuracy by getting the hue information at system start-up. A green frame is reflected on the screen at system start-up.

When this system starts, the information of the skin colour of the user can be acquired by putting a finger in the indicated green square. This can be detected by checking the occurring frequency of the hue value and using the threshold with the high occurring frequency. Thereby, the hue value of the background is not included.

In this system, the fingertips cannot be recognized only by hue information because an error in fingertip recognition might occur due to noise. The fingertip information is required to eliminate the error. The fingertip information is a fingertip image of the top of finger from the first joint of the finger. In this system, the information on a fingertip also can acquired when information with the colour of the user's skin is acquired.

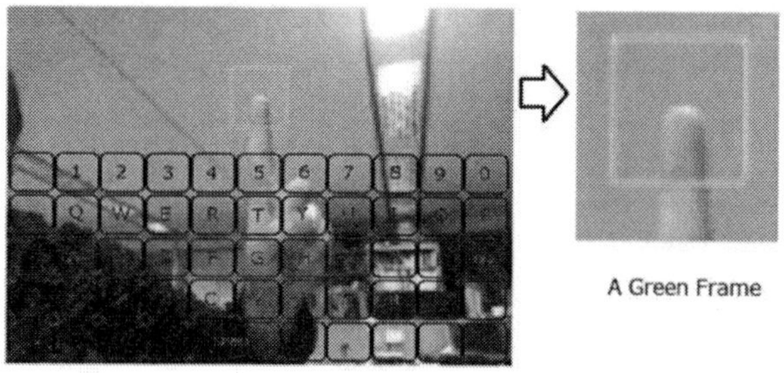

Figure 2. Screen of getting user data; A green frame is reflected on the screen at system start-up

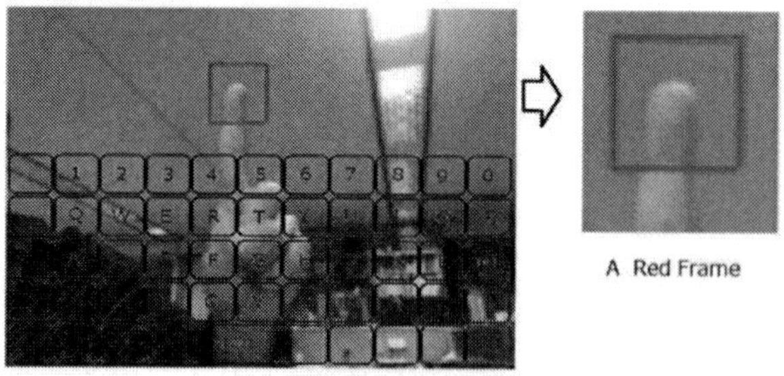

Figure 3. Screen of Recognized Finger of Character Input

Figure 4. An example of inputted key "I" by fingertip recognition

C. Recognition of the Fingertip

This system uses two methods to recognize the fingertip. The first is template matching using the fingertip information. The second is how to find the hue of a certain area of skin in the region.

Fig. 4 shows an example of keyboard input by the recognition of fingertip. The "I" key was selected by the red square.

This system uses template matching to detect a user's fingertip. Template matching is a technique in digital image processing for finding small parts of an image, which match a template image. A template image uses the fingertip image of the user. The calculation uses zero mean normalized cross-correlation (Fig. 5). Therefore, it is possible to stably calculate variations in brightness. As a result of the calculation, the lowest point of the value is the fingertip of a candidate. However, the point does not determine the fingertip.

At the second step, the hue of the skin in the specific area can be searched. The part recognized as a fingertip can be searched by template matching. When the skin colour of the region exceeds the fixed value, its location is the fingertips.

In the present system, we must have the skin colour threshold for fingertip recognition. Below describes a method for determining the threshold value. First, we perform fingertip recognition in the 30–40% threshold for the fingertips candidate. We perform the fingertip recognition 10 times in each threshold. Next, the threshold is increased by 10%. The threshold is recognized up to 80–90%. Table 2 is the number of successful recognitions in each threshold. From Table 2, we set the threshold to 50%–60%.

D. Using a Keyboard for the Input of a Character

This system uses the keyboard input method. Originally, the keyboard input method can input characters by pressing the keys. In this system, a fingertip reflected by the camera inputs a character by the user touching the virtual keyboard. Therefore it's necessary to decide touching time between a fingertip and a virtual keyboard. A decision procedure of touching time of a fingertip and a virtual keyboard is described in next sentence.

The letters "abcdefghijklnmopqrstuvwxyz" are entered in this system. The touching time of character input is 0.5, 1.0, 1.5 and 2.0 seconds. We measure the number of erroneous inputs and the input time. Table 3 is the result of each number of seconds.

From Table 3, we set the touching time to 1 second. It's because in case of 0.5 seconds there is many input error, and input time is too long in case of 1.5 seconds and 2.0 seconds.

$$\bar{T} = \frac{\sum_{j=0}^{N-1}\sum_{i=0}^{M-1} T(i,j)}{MN} \qquad \bar{I} = \frac{\sum_{j=0}^{N-1}\sum_{i=0}^{M-1} I(i,j)}{MN}$$

$$R_{ZNCC} = \frac{\sum_{j=0}^{N-1}\sum_{i=0}^{M-1}\left(\left(I(i,j)-\bar{I}\right)\left(T(i,j)-\bar{T}\right)\right)}{\sqrt{\sum_{j=0}^{N-1}\sum_{i=0}^{M-1}\left(I(i,j)-\bar{I}\right)^2 \times \sum_{j=0}^{N-1}\sum_{i=0}^{M-1}\left(T(i,j)-\bar{T}\right)^2}}$$

n = Template image of height, m = Template image of height
Search pixel = (i , j)
I (i , j) = Brightness Value of Input Image,
T(i , j) = Brightness Value of Template Image

Ī = Average Brightness Value of Input Image
T̄ = Average Brightness Value of Template Image

Figure 5. Zero mean normalized cross correlation

TABLE II. RELATED PAPERS OF CHARACTER INPUT METHOD

Skin Color Threshold (%)	30 -40	40 - 50	50 - 60	60 - 70	70 -80	80 - 90
No. of Successful Recognition	0	2	9	2	0	0

III. EXPERIMENT AND RESULTS

In this paper, we perform three experiments. The first experiment evaluates the accuracy of fingertip recognition. In this experiment, subjects performs the input 10 times for the letters from "a" to "z". In the second part of of the experiment, subjects input the phrase "university of aizu". After inputting, the subjects evaluate five items in five levels. We evaluate the utility of the system for each item. By two experiments, we evaluate the accuracy of fingertip recognition and keyboard input, the utility of the system. We use Apple's iPad 2 in the experiment. Device performance is described in Table 4.

A. Experiment of Finger Recognition

In this experiment, subjects perform the input 10 times for letters from "a" to "z". Experiments are performed in the situations of Fig. 6. Subjects are 30 cm away from the device. When a subject enters a character, the subject releases the finger from the virtual keyboard.

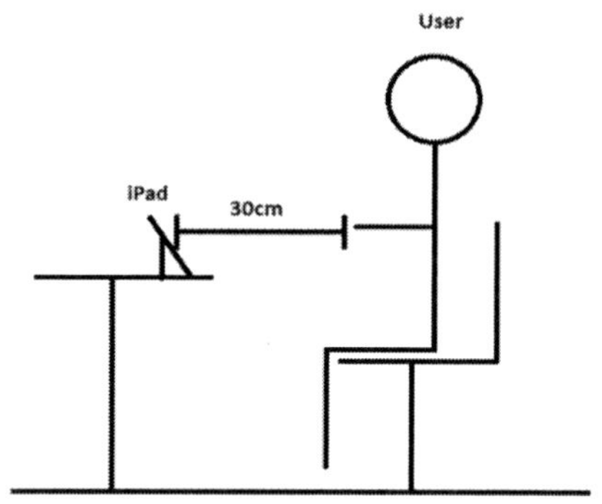

Figure 6. Simulation of Experiment

TABLE III. EXPERIMENT OF TOUCHING TIME THRESHOLD

Touching Time (second)	0.5	1.0	1.5	2.0
Input Time (second)	33	40	60	154
Erroneous Input	13	2	0	0

TABLE IV. PERFORMANCE OF IPAD 2

CPU	GPU	Memory	Camera
Apple A5 Dual Core Processor 1GHz	Power VR SGX543MP2 Dual Core Processor	512MB LPDDR2 RAM	VGA Image quality Max 30fps

TABLE V. EVALUATION ITEM

Evaluation Item	Explanation
Learnability	Users can easily use the System.
Efficiency	Users can achieve efficient purposes.
Memorability	Users do not forget how to use the system.
Errors	The system is a low incidence of error. Users can be easily addressed error.
Satisfaction	Users are satisfied with the system. Users can use without stress.

This experiment is to measure the recognition rate of each letter. As a result, we will evaluate the accuracy of fingertip recognition.

B. *Experiment of Performance Evaluation*

In the experiment, the subjects enter the phrase "university of aizu". The experiment will be performed on the condition shown as Fig. 6. After entering the phrase, the use evaluates the system as 5 steps for each of 5 items such as Learnability, Efficiency, Memorability, Errors, Satisfaction. Evaluation items refer to Jakob Nielsen [13].

From this experimental result, we measure the utility of this system.

TABLE VI. RESULT OF FINGERTIP RECOGNITION

Character	a	b	c	d	e	f
Detection Accuracy (%)	97	96	98	100	100	100

g	h	I	j	k	l	n	m	o	p
100	100	100	100	100	98	96	97	100	99

q	r	s	t	u	v	w	x	y	z
100	100	100	99	100	97	100	98	100	96

IV. DISCUSSION

From Table 6, the average input accuracy of the characters is 98.96%. The highest recognition rate is 100%, and the lowest recognition rate of character (b, m, z) is 96%. For research of character input using a virtual keyboard [4], the recognition rate average is 66%. Moreover, research using a smart device [14] has a recognition rate of 87% to 93%. Research of the character input gesture in Kinect [1] is the character input of Japanese. As a result, the recognition rate of each character is 50% to 100%, and the recognition accuracy is 86%. Our research obtained the better results than these studies.

This system is used for recognition of colours of objects and faces. For this reason, this system can recognize objects that are not a fingertip. There are three causes of error. First, we get the user's information in advance. However, there is a case that cannot be successfully acquired. The reason is that the image quality of the camera is low. This system can use a video image with the size of 1280 x 720 pixels. However, in this paper, we are using a video image of 192 vertical pixels × 144 horizontal pixels for the weight of the program. Therefore, there is a possibility of obtaining an incorrect user's hue value.

Secondly, when the user moves the finger quickly, the camera may not recognize the movement of the fingertip. This is caused by the specs of the device. The device used in the experiment is the iPad 2. The OS initially installed is iOS 4.3. However, the OS used in the experiment is iOS9. Therefore, the device does not have enough performance. To solve this problem, it is necessary to change the device used in the experiments to a newer device.

The third reason is the face as reflected on the screen. The hue information of the fingertips and the face is almost the same value. When the fingertip and the face are far away, the fingertip is recognized correctly. However, when the fingertip overlaps with the face or when the fingertip is near the face, the fingertip is not recognized correctly (Fig. 7). To solve this problem, it is necessary to separately recognize the fingertip and face by using depth. However, it is difficult to recognize depth in a smart device.

From Fig.8, the average of each evaluation item is 4.58. The highest item, "Memorability", is 4.9. "Learnability" is a high item, second at 4.8. (These are very good results compared with the result of input method using cell-phone [15]) With this result, it is considered very easy to use system for users by employing the keyboard input method. It was able to reduce the burden of the input method.

However, "Efficiency" was 4.1. This is the lowest result for the evaluation items. This is because, when the user moves the finger quickly, the camera may not recognize the movement of the fingertip.

In addition, when the user inputs a character, the fingertip requires contact with the virtual keyboard for a certain period of time. Therefore, character input is slowed down. However, "Satisfaction" is 4.6. This value is not low. From this result, we understand that users use the system with less stress.

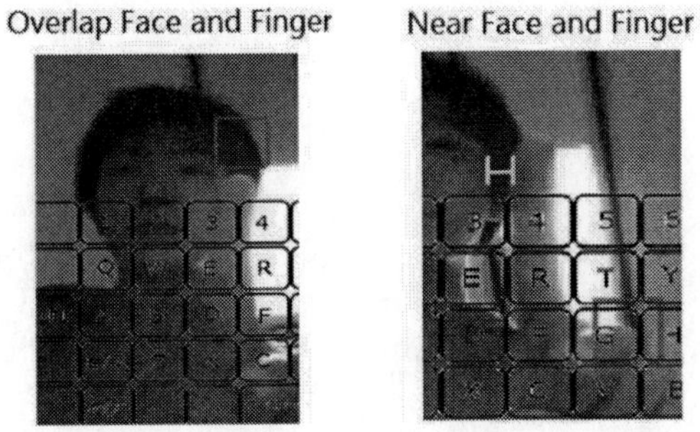

Figure 7. The error cases of finger.

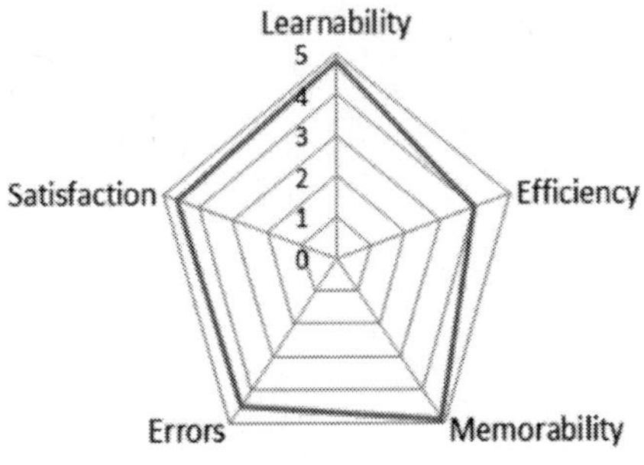

Figure 8. Result of Performance Evaluation

V. CONCLUSION

This paper has three purposes. First, users can input characters regardless of the location and the environment. Second, users can input characters without special tools. Last, users can input characters without touching the screen by using this system. Therefore, users can input characters at a remote location. Character input by fingertips by using the smart device has a high precision with an average of 98.96% for each character. In addition, users use this system and users evaluate five items in five levels. As a result, we obtain an evaluation of the average at 4.58.

We did fingertip detection using a smart device. Then, we made character input from a long distance possible by a virtual keyboard. We did not use special tools. Then, we input a character, and the character input did not depend on the environment and location. Therefore, we were able to obtain high practicality.

As future works, first the initial camera change mode will be developed for more comfortable use. Second the model to support multi-finger input (e.g., when using the two hands) will be developed, as users on smart devices strive to be more and more efficient in text messaging.

REFERENCES

[1] O. Masato and M. Sou, "KooSHO: Japanese Input Environment Based on the Handwriting Gestures in the Air," The Association for Natural Language Processing, Proceedings of the NAACL HLT 2013 Demonstration Session, pp. 24–27, Atlanta, Georgia, June 2013.

[2] K. Hosono, M. Sasakura, H. Tanabe, and T. Kawakami, "A proposal of the character input method by gesture operation using Leap Motion," The 28th Annual Conference of the Japanese Society for Artificial Intelligence, pp. 1-4, 2014.

[3] M. Fujimoto, M. Imura, Yoshihiro Yasumuro, and Yoshitsugu Manabe, Kunihiro Chihara, "AirGrabber : vlrtual keyboard using miniature camera and tilt sensor," The Virtual Reality Society of Japan (TVRSJ), vol. 9, no. 4, pp. 413-422, 2004.

[4] N. Matsui and Y. Yamamoto, "Virtual Keyboard: Realization of Robust Real-Time Fingertip Detection from Video-Image," Proc. SPA2000, Japan Society for Software Science and Technology, 2000-3, pp. 1- 7, 2001 (in Japanese).

[5] M. Weiss, R. Jennings, J. Wagner, R. Khoshabeh, J. D. Hollan, and J. Borchers, "SLAP: silicone illuminated active peripherals," Medical Computing Group, ITS 08. 2008.

[6] Y. Nishida and T. Yoshida, "A research for aerial handwritten gesture recognition with Kinect interaction", Memoirs of the Fukui Institute of Technology, No. 440, pp. 25-30, 2014.

[7] M. Kaneko and M. Iwata, "Proposal and implementation of T9-Flick Keyboard on tablet devices screen", Tokyo Conference of Institute of Electronics, Information, and Communication Engineers, D-6, pp. 223, 2015.

[8] S. Takahiro, M. Yoshiaki, "Smartphones text input system", SIG Technical Report, Information Processing Society of Japan, Vol. 2013, No.3, pp. 1-6, 2013.

[9] R. Yamamoto and H. Miyashita, "Operation and authentication of smart phone by earphone", Internal Conference of Information Processing Society of Japan (Interaction 2013), pp. 626-631, 2013.

[10] T. Aoki, M. Nomura, H. Tamura, "Finger language recognition using the RGB-D camera", Internal Conference of Information Processing Society of Japan, 4ZB-3, pp.187-188, 2013.

[11] Y. Orimo, Y. Tamakuni, Daisuke Takahashi, and Noriyoshi Okamoto, "An experiment on finger spelling recognition by using Kinect," The Institute of Image Information and Television Engineers, ITE Technical Report, Vol. 38, No. 9, pp. 31-32, Feb. 2014.

[12] K. Watanabe, Y. Iwai, Yasushi Yagi, and Masahiko Yachida, "Gesture recognition using a colored glove," Institute of Electronics, Information, and Communication Engineers, vol.1, No. 25, pp.662-666 Aug 1996.

[13] J. Nielsen, 2002, "Usability engineering," Morgan Kaufmann, 1993.

[14] A. Tatsuya, T. Jirou, and Mimatsu Kazuo, "Smartphones input method based on magnetic," University of Tsukuba, Master's thesis, 2015.

[15] Y. Masato, "A study of the software key input method of the operation device for the information weak," Thesis for a degree in University of Kouchi, 2004.

Hide, Don't Seek: on User-Centric Location Accuracy

Marta Piekarska
Technische Universität Berlin
Berlin, Germany
Email: marta@sec.t-labs.tu-berlin.de

Abstract—**Location Privacy has been a very attractive topic for the past years. The amount of location blurring, hiding and privacy preserving solutions proposed by the researchers is very big. The number of such services implemented on the market, however, is quite small. Moreover, the ones actually used by the people is close to zero. We see this gap as very troubling. With the spread of devices that will allow for tracking users - the smartwatches, connected medical devices, smartphones and fitness trackers, location privacy will become even more important. When the devices become connected into the Internet of Things, so that it will be hardly possible to escape tracking: already today 70% of users sleep with their phones next to their beds. In our work, we approached the problem from a user-centric perspective, developed our solution together with users and learned what are their expectations towards such a feature.**

Keywords–mobile privacy; location accuracy; user-centric privacy.

I. Introduction

Location based services (LBS) use the information about the geographical position of a mobile device to enhance the quality of experience (QoE) of the user. There are common use cases to which users may be completely oblivious to, for example geotags in images taken by the phone camera. There is a flip side of the LBS. From a privacy perspective exposing the location data to a third-party poses a serious threat. Once the location information leaves a device it may be subject to interception, improper handling, leakage or sale. That causes users' discomfort [1], which has led to development of the European Directive on Privacy and Electronic Communications and decision that location-based services must be permission-based [2]. This means that the end user should opt-in to the service in order to use it.

As recently presented, users identify three discomforts connected to usage of mobile devices: feeling in control, ease of use and ability to take actions [3]. Currently, none of the available mobile OSes introduces any kind of fine grained, flexible control of the location data. In Android one has to accept access to geolocation during installation. In iOS, the user is prompted in real-time, but the only choice she can make is a binary one. Neither of the solutions deals with the concerns found in [3].

We approached the problem from a user-centric perspective and present the results in the paper. We contribute with our work on the following levels:

- Improved location obfuscation based on the grid algorithm.
- Location Privacy preserving solution using a user-centric method
- Very high fliexbility of the solution
- Presentation of user-study and lessons learned from the development of the solution.

The rest of the paper is organized as follows. We start in the next section by evaluating the work done in the field. In Section III, the general solution is presented, which we later improve through the use of a user-centric approach. Results of these consultations and user expectations are described in Section IV. Afterwards we focus on the lessons that can be learned from our work through user-study evaluation and technical analysis. We present the findings and action points that come out from those in Section V. We finish with conclusions in Section VI.

II. Evaluation of Existing Solutions

Technological Aspects Minami and Borisov provide a formal definition of location privacy and suggest a possible solution to the problem in [4]. Andre et al. show another approach where they formalize the intuitive notion of protecting the user's location within a radius r with a level of privacy that depends on r, in [5]. Their work can be generalized to a version of differential privacy. A recent work of Shokri et al. [6] tries to formalize the location–based application, model various location–privacy preserving mechanisms and establish an analytical framework, based on Bayesian inference in Hidden Markov Processes. For more work on privacy preserving systems interested reader should also look into [7]. We have used those works as the background to understand the problem of location obfuscation.

A popular measure of location privacy is the k–anonymity, where we consider a position as hidden if it is indistinguishable from k–1 other users in the same region. First works were done by Gruteser et al [8] where they have proposed to discuss the cloaking region defined as a Quad-tree. Another variant of the same approach was presented in New Casper by Mokbel et al in [9]. Other works introducing the same concept include [10], [11] or [12]. Work of Ahamed et al. [13] attempts to deal with the biggest problem of the k–anonymity - most frameworks use a Location Anonymizer, which is a trusted third-party (TTP) that can define how many people are in a region. Another proposal on how to replace the TTP was given by Ristenpart et al. in [14]. Here, authors suggest using OpenDHT as the third party service for tracking lost and stolen devices. An OpenDHT is a distributed hash table server that has been described in [15]. Any k–anonymity approaches have been proven weak and rather useless by Diaz in [16]. After careful analysis of the approaches to location obfuscation we have decided to use the grid method, as the most convenient one and not requiring any TTP. It also did not introduce any computing overhead.

Apps More generic permission controlling frameworks have been proposed for Android. Nauman et al. developed a very extensive policy enforcement framework that removes the problem of binary permission granting [17]. Within the scope of their work they give the user a possibility of restraining access to location while preserving the ability of the application to work. Another work in the general field of policy enforcement is CRePE [18]. It is a context–related policy enforcement for Android and can be used to define fine-grained policies. Examples of leveraging the role-based access control include DR BACA [19] and CtRBAC [20]. A different approach is taken in MockDroid [21]. Here authors modify the OS in such a way that the user can "mock" the applications access to the resources. Similar approach has been proposed in AppFence [22]. Zhou et al. propose a flexible, dynamic control of fine–grained permissions in different scenarios with TISSA [23]. Market Place applications that allow the users to block access to location [21] or use fake location [24], are not done on the system level, and suffer from big usability problems.

Psychology Research by Fu and Lindqvust [25] gives an understanding of the problem from more psychological perspective. They evaluated how people understand Android's location permissions and how will users' behavior change after we educate them on their true meaning. In [26] Tsai et al. evaluate the peoples' perception of the location sharing cost to benefit ratio by an online survey. They found that respondents feel that the risks of using location-sharing technologies outweigh the advantages. When building a privacy preserving solution, it is often assumed that, in order to improve the users' practices, they should be presented with the possibility of setting a small number of privacy profiles, which can provide basis for configuring individual preferences. According to the study presented in [27], however, this approach can encourage users to share significantly more without a substantial difference in comfort. Based on their three week study, Benisch et al [28], describe a methodology for quantifying the effects, in terms of accuracy and amount of sharing, of privacy-setting types with differing levels of complexity. Other works on the factors impacting users' decision to give away information can be found in [29] and [30]. All of the above gave us understanding of the mindset of the users and led us to designing a system with the choice of per-app setting with various adjustment mechanisms.

III. General Solution

As presented in Figure 1, we introduce four different ways to deal with an LBS. User, as always, can give to the app his precise position, or decide to turn the location services off. However, we also give him the possibility of meeting privacy half way - by either adjusting the granularity of the position, or completely faking it. Because the feature is not part of the prompt window, but an element of its own in the Settings, user can always go back and change her choice.

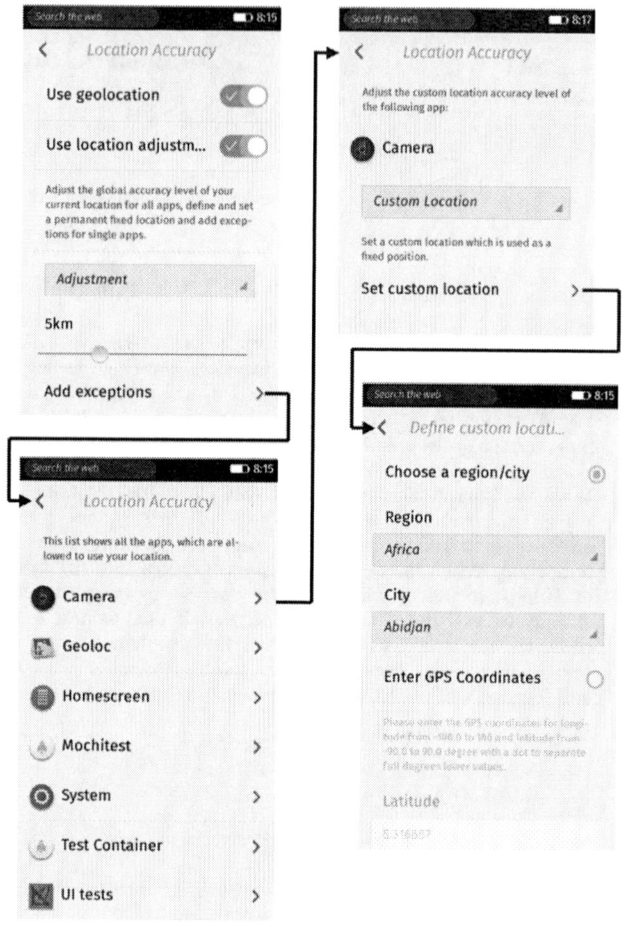

Figure 1. Flow of the Extended Location Settings

1) Faking the location: There are many situations in life where we do not want to reveal where we are. Unfortunately, this is not something an LBS will accept: either the application will stop working or it will not even get installed. In addition to that, when one wants to access a service from a location that does not allow for it - certain web pages or shops will only work in a given country. Thus faking your position to the region that is actually acceptable by the app, will extend the functionality. We provide two methods of faking the position. The user can either choose from a predefined set of continents and major cities, where the coordinates are set to the center of the city. The second method is entering position by hand, to allow for precise setting. Figure 2 provides a close–up view of the choice screen.

2) Adjusting the accuracy: Going one step towards usability, we have also implemented a mechanism that allows to change the granularity of information shared with the app. As [31] has showed, people have much less concern when only obfuscated location is revealed. We have designed our "Adjustable Location Accuracy" setting, so that it adds necessary noise to the precise position and returns values that are within the limits set by the user for a given app. After obtaining precise location from the available sensors, we use an obfuscation method to provide a certain level of uncertainty.

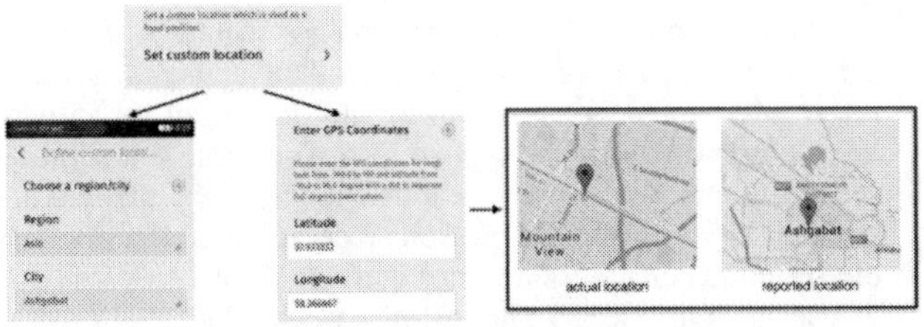

Figure 2. Fixed location setting.

Figure 3. Approximating the position with a grid algorithm

The fuzzing is realized by introducing a grid, where each cell is of the dimensions chosen by the user. The coordinates are used to determine the square in which she currently is. Then we find the middle point of that cell and return that to the application. The visualization of the process is presented in Figure 3. Similar algorithm was first proposed by Micinski et al in [32].

As we deal with a sphere and cartesian coordinates, it has to be taken into account that the size of the grid will change towards the poles. We thus use separate equations to calculate the latitude and longitude. For the latitude, we simplify the calculations by assuming a fixed radius of the earth halfway between the poles and the equator. It is calculated from the radius at 45 degrees North.

First we need to convert the precise latitude into the universal polar stereographic (UPS) coordinate system, so that it accounts for the ellipsoid changes. Next, we find the southern edge of the grid cell, in radians, and add half of a grid cell size to find the center latitude. Lastly, we need to convert the calculation back to degrees, properly wrap it back and return the value in degrees. An ellipsoid with semi–major axis A and semi–minor axis B, has a variable radius at an angle of latitude, ϕ.

3) Implementing per-app Settings: The system is designed to have a single global value, and optionally, a setting per-origin (i.e., per-app). If a geolocation request comes in from an origin that does not have an origin-specific setting, the global setting is used. But this system presents a problem since the existing geolocation system tracked requests by "watch ID" instead of origin. The relationship between origin and watch ID is many-to-one; each origin can have multiple watches set up and running. The geolocation subsystem assigns an unique watch ID for each active geolocation request. Updates from the positioning system come in and then get reported, unchanged, back to the owner of the request. To apply the correct fuzzing behavior, we required a way to get the current fuzzing settings for the origin associated with a given watch ID. We accomplished this by recording the origin in a hash table whenever a new watch ID was generated and clearing the mapping whenever a request was destroyed and the watch ID invalidated.

4) Implementation of Various Levels of Precision: For the "precise location" setting, the behavior is exactly the same as before; the location data is sent directly to the requesting origin without modification. The "fixed location" setting is straightforward. Regardless of what geolocation data come from the sensors, we report the user settable fixed location to the requesting code.

For the "no location" setting, we just destroy the location data and report nothing. To maintain expected behavior for the W3C geolocation API, we had to allow app code to request a geolocation watch and get one, but there is no standardized value for "no location" so we chose to just prevent any data from getting reported.

The most difficult setting to implement is the approximate, fuzzed location. We created a class to encapsulate the fuzzing behavior. We implemented the WGS84 geodetic system for the earth ellipsoid. The constants chosen come from [33]. To simplify the calculations we assumed a fixed radius of the earth at 45 degrees north latitude, and the longitudinal radius was based on a given longitude.

There are attacks against the algorithm we have used. When the user is moving, it can be observed over time how he changes the cells, thus the probability of revealing his location from a square, drops to a linear one. Moreover, if the attacker will take the road map of a given region and compares it with the data collected, the cloaking ratio drops to $\frac{1}{No.of roads}$. To reduce the probability of succeeding, we introduce a jitter when the device is moving. This will not remove the possibility of performing the attack. It will, however, introduce additional level of uncertainty. Based on the speed we include a random delay with which the position is being changed.

IV. User Expectation

After creating a simple prototype of a location preserving solution that would allow for adjusting location accuracy, we have worked with a group of "every day experts" – users who are not technically savvy towards improving and building a solution that would meet their expectation. We used the user-centric approach discussed in [3]. From that we have found that we should provide users with ability to set different levels of settings for different applications, add contextual dependencies and create profiles. We describe those concepts below.

A. *Application–transparent obfuscation*

On the first level a user is asked to define the global, system-wide setting, that will be the default choice for any app. In addition, one can create a list of applications that will be subject to different adjustment.

The apps can be grouped by vendor, sorted alphabetically or by the trust level. By the latter we refer to the definition of "web", "privileged", and "certified". Moreover, the user can just search for the applications by name. We give the users choice of such filtering to help them with making the decision on how much do they trust the applications. By allowing to group apps by vendor name user can see which of them may potentially collaborate. Sorting based on system's definition of trust gives intuition about the risk of potential maliciousness of an app. Additional ways to improve that mechanism would be adjusting the location granularity based on the application type. However, Firefox OS currently does not provide information that would allow for such grouping.

B. Adding the Context to Decision Making

In addition to per-app setting we introduce another level of definition. Following the concepts presented in other fields, our solution gives the user a choice of setting both temporal and spatial intervals where chosen level of adjustment will be set. This means that now the user can define time span and space where the location granularity will be changed. This solution is useful when entering the area or time slot of increased privacy - being in a hospital or during the night.

C. Creating Profiles

In addition to above–mentioned extensions we also decided to include user profiles. Following the conclusion that there are situations where one might want to switch into a stealthy mode, or quite the opposite - for the time being needs all applications to access everything - we allow users to save their settings into profiles. This way they can adjust the granularity ahead of time and activate the mode when needed. Such setting, of course, can be time consuming and tiresome. It is however an option, and not a requirement, and can be done at any given point in time. The profiles can also be activated based on temporal and spatial information.

V. Lessons Learned

One of the biggest contributions of this work is a summary of lessons learned while implementing the design with a user-centric approach and setting out clear action points how to improve the location protecting solutions.

A. User-study Evaluation

The scope of the user-study evaluation was to verify the impact of our approach. Results presented here only reflect the evaluation of the solution. Additional findings, connected to what where the particular choices users made, how did they differentiate the applications, and how often did they change their configuration, will be further analyzed and presented in a later publication.

1) Methodology: The group consisted of 30 participants, 40% males and 60% females fairly equally distributed between 17 and 60 years old. Their educational background varied: 36,7% graduated from a collage, 30% were still in college, 20% had a higher education level like a master degree. The remaining group had either a high school diploma, or finished their education one level before that. These show, that there was a bias towards a higher education levels. The participants were distributed between all kinds of jobs: students, graphic designers, secretaries, clerks, lawyer assistants, project managers, etc. None of the participants have ever used Firefox OS, however all of them previously had a smartphone.

Each participant was invited to the lab, where they were handed the phone, and asked to use it as their primary device. They were not informed about the precise purpose of the study, but we have told them that their behavior would be monitored. Prior to the study, we have obtained their approval, promised the results would be anonymized and only used for research. We incorporated into the typical First-Time-Use run additional screens about the privacy features included in the modified system. The Adjustable Location Accuracy was described with the set of screens presented in Figure 4. We asked participants to use the Firefox OS phone for a week. We monitored and made sure that they were using the devices during the study.

2) Survey: After the test period finished we invited the participants back to the lab. We asked them to give their opinions on following statements:

1) I am satisfied with the Adjustable Location Accuracy.
2) I feel that using Adjustable Location Accuracy slows down my phone.
3) I feel that Adjustable Location Accuracy is a feature that was hard to use.
4) How often did you set up the Adjustable Location Accuracy?
5) Name setting that you found most useful.

For the first three questions participants were asked to choose one out of seven possible answers. We have based the choice on the Likert scale: 1 - Strongly disagree, 2 - Disagree, 3 - Somehow disagree, 4 - Neither agree nor disagree, 5 - Somehow agree, 6 - Agree, 7 - Strongly agree [34]. Question number 4 had the following answers possible: 1 - I did not use the feature at all, 2 - I have tried to setup the feature and resigned, 3 - I have setup the feature once, 4 - I have setup the feature repeatedly. In this question we asked the users to justify their answers in free–text response. Last question was multiple choice, limited to 3, with the following possibilities: 1 - I did not find Adjustable Location Accuracy useful at all, 2 - No location, 3 - Precise Location, 4 - Custom Location, 5 - Adjustment, 6 - Per-application settings, 7 - Global setting, 8 - Privacy Profiles. We also left space for free-text comments.

3) Results: First question was measuring the general satisfaction with the solution. 80% of the participants chose answer 6 and 7, which means they were highly satisfied with the functions provided, 13% chose "Somehow agree", and 7% were ambiguous about it (answer 4). None of the users reported lack of satisfaction. For the second question we have seen only answers that did not suggest any delays: 83% said that they strongly disagree with the statement, while 17% chose option 2. With the question number three we wanted to verify what was the perception of out tool. While most users said that they did not find the solution hard (40% Strongly disagree, 26.7% Disagree, 26.7% Neither Agree nor Disagree, 6.6% Somehow agree), in the comments section they have often mentioned that the process of setting up the tool was time consuming. However, when looking at the answers to question 4 we noticed that most users set up the process only once (20 people). 8 participants chose answer number 4, while only 2 participants did not use the feature at all. They argued they "did not feel like it changed anything". We did not verify if this was due to bad explanation in the Guided Tour or different privacy expectation. Lastly, the users chose mostly the "Privacy Profiles"(83.3%), "Custom Location" (76.7%), "Per application settings" (66.7%). These were followed by "Global Settings" (40%).

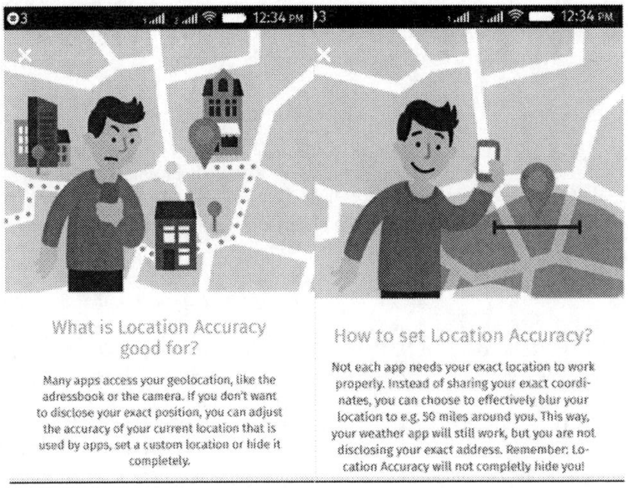

Figure 4. The first two wireframes presented to the participants of the user study performed to evaluate the adaptation of our framework.

Overall we saw that participants were happy to use the feature and did not notice any performance problems. We have concluded that users are happy to adapt Privacy Enhancing Technologies (PETs), as long as they do not have to give up usability. Because PETs do not offer users more features or a better experience, the best way to drive adoption is by making them both transparent and automatic. There is more to be done on the topic of user studies and user-perception of location accuracy. We plan to deeply investigate the topic, as the results to the last question were very interesting to us. We feel that our solution would benefit from an automated setting based on recommendations made by trusted people. However, this might not improve the privacy, as [27] suggests.

B. Technical Analysis

The location obfuscation does not include any overhead compared to lack of the feature. However to ensure higher impact, it requires to introduce some kind of IP randomization, which we will further discuss in Section V-C.

Our solution does not cause the apps to break and even enhances functionality. Some applications require the user to grant permission to access the geolocation data from the device. By reporting no location, the app receives access but doesn't get any location data that is useful for tracking the user. This empowers the user to gain access to the app without compromising their privacy. This is possible, because applications usually set up a callback to handle the location information once it is obtained from the system. When the user selects "no location", no data is returned and the callbacks never get called. If the application is designed to asynchronously handle location information updates, it usually continues to work and simply uses the IP-based position. The application will typically have a hierarchy of geolocation sources and the API based is highest in the rank. Thus with other settings, like "Adjustment", or "Custom Location" it will just accept the data returned by the Geolocation API.

C. Fighting IP-based Location

The biggest problem of any location obfuscation solution is the IP-based attack. We propose to fight against it by using a Tor-based solution [35]. In order to do that, some changes in the current implementation of Tor need to be done: the exit nodes should comply with the region chosen by the user location. Assume there are two web sites, A.com and B.com, that both use tracking cookies/images from C.com. If the user visits A.com with Tor and location obfuscation and B.com without Tor and location obfuscation, then C.com's tracking will see two different IP's and locations for the user. If the user then visits a third site with C.com tracking bits on it, then C.com will see the same IP and location data it saw when the user visited B.com. C.com can develop a statistical model for the location and IP of the user that will discount the masked IP and fuzzed location reported when accessing A.com. This problem can be addressed by developing a cookie management method for obfuscation techniques. Currently we believe that the best way this attack can be defeated is by applying the cookie policies found in the Tor Browser Bundle (TBB) and ensuring that all the traffic is forwarded through the Tor. We strongly encourage better investigation how Tor technologies can be incorporated into industry solutions.

D. W3C standard improvements

The W3C geolocation API takes into consideration the impact on user privacy in Section 4 of the specification [36]. It states that "a conforming implementation of [the] specification must provide a mechanism that protects the user's privacy...". They do not, however, specify how this should be done. Our implementation attempts to further improve basic geolocation with user selectable behavior of the geolocation discovery and reporting mechanism. Moreover we introduce the possibility of setting a custom chosen, fixed position. We believe that it should be an enhancement of the specification to introduce both the "no location" and "fixed position" choices. We do not suggest working on the fuzzing mechanism, as this has not been proven to be secure.

In case of the "custom location" there should be a requirement to allow the user to set the position to a defined value. This would comply with the request of respecting privacy that is not currently enforced. For the "no location" we would like to introduce a constant value. When a user selects the behavior in our implementation, we do not execute any position callbacks to the client application. In some cases, web apps interpret the lack of a callback as an error condition. This would not be the case if a constant was present that would define what "no location" is. Then we could execute the callback with that value and avoid the incorrect error condition. We propose that "no location" be represented by a position value of NaN for the coordinate latitude, longitude, and accuracy as well as a timestamp value of 0.

E. User-centric Lessons

Working together with the users from the very beginning gave us a good understanding of what people expect of a location obfuscation solution. As with other privacy enhancing technologies, user expect privacy preserving location based services to run in the background and somehow "intuitively guess" what would they want to reveal in any given moment. Consent to share location data with an app heavily depends on the context, be it spacial or temporal as presented in [37]. Defining static polices does not conform those requirements for the system. Thus when granting access to location not only should we ask the question of "if" but also "in what circumstances". In addition, extending this by adding per-app settings allows for further flexibility, while introducing profiles makes the management slightly easier. However the more flexible and adjustable the solution is the harder it gets to build a user interface for it. We definitely see this as a challenge to be further explored and investigated.

VI. Conclusions

In our work towards user–centric privacy, we developed a tool that is a compromise between hiding and usability. With various levels of protection, ranging from turning the LBS off, through providing a fake location, adjusted accuracy all the way to precise position. By including the Guided Tour that explains the feature we educate the user on threats connected to revealing his data and give him opportunity to protect it according to his needs and concerns. We have developed our code on Firefox OS, and tested it on physical devices. The overhead is unnoticeable by the users, as we have presented. Moreover, our user study showed that people do not feel discomfort while adjusting the settings initially. They rather report it is a good way to learn which apps access their location data .We would like to investigate more carefully how can we comply with the six goals suggested publication of Luo and Hengartner [38]. We would also want to analyze a very different concept described by Puttaswamy and Zhao [39] - where the external servers are treated as simple encrypted data stores. This removes the problem of leaking any data to anyone but the parties directly involved. We think that our solution could greatly benefit from this addition. The proposed scheme is a solution to the concerns users have around the location privacy. It is flexible, which gives good QoE. The idea of adjusting location on per–app basis, takes into account the context - users will be willing to share different things with different applications. It is adjustable straight in the settings, so that depending on the situations they can also change their choice. By grouping the apps with respect to their vendor, we give the overview of which apps may be collaborating with each other, which has not yet been seen as an attack vector. The elements of context–awareness and pre-setting profiles make it even more user–centric.

We have identified several action points for the academia and the industry. First is better support of user-centric development of privacy tools in general, and location privacy preserving solutions especially. We strongly believe that this is the only way to get the adaptation rate of PETs higher. Second is improving the current W3C geolocation standard by introducing the "no location" solution. Additionally the geofencing document should be designed with grater care. We see a problem in the fact that the whole drafted before the actual Privacy section was written. Taking into account how sensitive already is the location data, and what the API would allow for it is troubling. The great lesson learned from working together with the users on privacy enhancing technologies is seeing how they care about their data, and protecting it, however they seek solutions that are transparent and intuitive. We believe that it is the role of the standardization bodies and academia to work together towards creating such standards.

References

[1] S. Patil, G. Norcie, A. Kapadia, and A. Lee, ""check out where i am!": Location-sharing motivations, preferences, and practices," in *CHI '12 Extended Abstracts on Human Factors in Computing Systems*.

[2] "Directive on privacy and electronic communications," European Parliament, Tech. Rep., 12 July 2002.

[3] M. Piekarska, Y. Zhou, D. Strohmeier, and A. Raake, "Because we care: Privacy dashboard on firefox os," in *Web 2.0 Security and Privacy 2015, S&P IEEE.*

[4] K. Minami and N. Borisov, "Protecting location privacy against inference attacks," in *Proceedings of the 9th Annual ACM Workshop on Privacy in the Electronic Society*, ser. WPES '10.

[5] M. E. Andrés, N. E. Bordenabe, K. Chatzikokolakis, and C. Palamidessi, "Geo-indistinguishability: Differential privacy for location-based systems," *CoRR*, 2012.

[6] R. Shokri, G. Theodorakopoulos, J.-Y. Le Boudec, and J.-P. Hubaux, "Quantifying location privacy," in *Security and Privacy (SP), 2011 IEEE Symposium on*, 2011.

[7] M. Herrmann, C. Troncoso, C. Diaz, and B. Preneel, "Optimal sporadic location privacy preserving systems in presence of bandwidth constraints," in *Proceedings of the 12th ACM Workshop on Workshop on Privacy in the Electronic Society*, ser. WPES '13.

[8] M. Gruteser and D. Grunwald, "Anonymous usage of location-based services through spatial and temporal cloaking," in *Proceedings of the 1st International Conference on Mobile Systems, Applications and Services*, ser. MobiSys '03.

[9] M. F. Mokbel, C.-Y. Chow, and W. G. Aref, "The new casper: Query processing for location services without compromising privacy," in *Proceedings of the 32Nd International Conference on Very Large Data Bases*, ser. VLDB '06.

[10] M. Jang, M. Yoon, H.-i. Kim, and J.-W. Chang, "A privacy-aware location cloaking technique reducing bandwidth consumption in location-based services," in *Proceedings of the Third ACM SIGSPATIAL International Workshop on Querying and Mining Uncertain Spatio-Temporal Data*, ser. QUeST '12.

[11] H. Elmeleegy, M. Ouzzani, A. Elmagarmid, and A. Abusalah, "Preserving privacy and fairness in peer-to-peer data integration," in *Proceedings of the 2010 ACM SIGMOD International Conference on Management of Data*.

[12] A. Solanas, F. Sebé, and J. Domingo-Ferrer, "Micro-aggregation-based heuristics for p-sensitive k-anonymity: One step beyond," in *Proceedings of the 2008 International Workshop on Privacy and Anonymity in Information Society*.

[13] S. I. Ahamed, C. S. Hasan, M. M. Haque, and M. O. Gani, "Towards ttp-free lightweight solution for location privacy using location-based anonymity prediction," in *Proceedings of the 2011 ACM Symposium on Research in Applied Computation*.

[14] T. Ristenpart, G. Maganis, A. Krishnamurthy, and T. Kohno, "Privacy-preserving location tracking of lost or stolen devices: Cryptographic techniques and replacing trusted third parties with dhts," in *Proceedings of the 17th Conference on Security Symposium*, ser. SS'08.

[15] S. Rhea, B. Godfrey, B. Karp, J. Kubiatowicz, S. Ratnasamy, S. Shenker, I. Stoica, and H. Yu, "Opendht: A public dht service and its uses," 2005.

[16] C. Diaz, "A closer look at cloaking techniques for location privacy," in *Katholieke Universiteit Leuven*, 2010.

[17] M. Nauman, S. Khan, and X. Zhang, "Apex: Extending android permission model and enforcement with user-defined runtime constraints," ser. ASIACCS '10.

[18] M. Conti, V. T. N. Nguyen, and B. Crispo, "Crepe: Context-related policy enforcement for android," ser. ISC'10.

[19] F. Rohrer, Y. Zhang, L. Chitkushev, and T. Zlateva, "Dr baca: Dynamic role based access control for android," ser. ACSAC '13.

[20] T. T. W. Yee and N. Thein, "Leveraging access control mechanism of android smartphone using context-related role-based access control model," in *Networked Computing and Advanced Information Management (NCM), 2011 7th International Conference on*.

[21] A. R. Beresford, A. Rice, N. Skehin, and R. Sohan, "Mockdroid: Trading privacy for application functionality on smartphones," ser. HotMobile '11.

[22] P. Hornyack, S. Han, J. Jung, S. Schechter, and D. Wetherall, "These aren't the droids you're looking for: Retrofitting android to protect data from imperious applications," ser. CCS '11.

[23] Y. Zhou, X. Zhang, X. Jiang, and V. W. Freeh, "Taming information-stealing smartphone applications (on android)," ser. TRUST'11.

[24] "http://www.placemask.com/products."

[25] H. Fu and J. Lindqvist, "General area or approximate location?: How people understand location permissions," in *Proceedings of the 13th Workshop on Privacy in the Electronic Society*, ser. WPES '14.

[26] J. Y. Tsai, P. G. Kelley, L. F. Cranor, and N. Sadeh, "Location-sharing technologies: Privacy risks and controls," in *A Journal of Law and Policy for the Information Society 6(2)*, 2010.

[27] S. Wilson, J. Cranshaw, N. Sadeh, A. Acquisti, L. F. Cranor, J. Springfield, S. Y. Jeong, and A. Balasubramanian, "Privacy manipulation and acclimation in a location sharing application," in *Proceedings of the 2013 ACM International Joint Conference on Pervasive and Ubiquitous Computing*.

[28] M. Benisch, P. G. Kelley, N. Sadeh, and L. F. Cranor, "Capturing location-privacy preferences: Quantifying accuracy and user-burden tradeoffs," *Personal Ubiquitous Comput.*

[29] S. Patil, Y. Le Gall, A. J. Lee, and A. Kapadia, "My privacy policy: Exploring end-user specification of free-form location access rules," in *Proceedings of the 16th International Conference on Financial Cryptography and Data Security*.

[30] J. Y. Tsai, P. Kelley, P. Drielsma, L. F. Cranor, J. Hong, and N. Sadeh, "Who's viewed you?: The impact of feedback in a mobile location-sharing application," in *Proceedings of the SIGCHI Conference on Human Factors in Computing Systems*, 2009.

[31] K. Fawaz and K. G. Shin, "Location privacy protection for smartphone users," in *Proceedings of the 2014 ACM SIGSAC Conference on Computer and Communications Security*.

[32] K. Micinski, P. Phelps, and J. S. Foster, "An Empirical Study of Location Truncation on Android," in *Mobile Security Technologies (MoST) 2013*.

[33] N. G.-I. Agency, *World Geodetic System 1984*.

[34] I. Allen and C. A. Seaman, "Likert scales and data analyses,," *Quality Progress, vol. 40, no. 7*, 2007.

[35] "Tor project." [Online]. Available: www.torproject.org

[36] W3C, "Geo api specification." [Online]. Available: http://dev.w3.org/geo/api/spec-source.html

[37] S. Consolvo, I. E. Smith, T. Matthews, A. LaMarca, J. Tabert, and P. Powledge, "Location disclosure to social relations: Why, when, & what people want to share," ser. CHI '05.

[38] W. Luo and U. Hengartner, "Proving your location without giving up your privacy," ser. HotMobile '10.

[39] K. P. N. Puttaswamy and B. Y. Zhao, "Preserving privacy in location-based mobile social applications," ser. HotMobile '10.

Light Reflection Spectrum Comparison of Pesticides Free Foods, Organic Foods and Conventional Farming Foods for VIS NIR Filter Creation

Oumy Diop
Antibes, France,
Email : diop.oumydiop@gmail.com

Umberto Cerasani
CERAGOS Electronics and Nature
Sophia Antipolis, France
Email: cerasani@ceragos.org

***Abstract*— A method for determination of food contaminants, including pesticides, is described in this document. Using Visible Near InfraRed spectroscopy results obtained from food samples with different levels of pollution, the creation of pesticides free food filters were realized. Methodology and data extraction are meticulously addressed. Finally, implementation of these filters in an embedded device, communicating with smartphone application is discussed allowing users to monitor food contaminants.**

Keywords—pesticides; organic farming; Vis NIR spectroscopy; filter creation; data collection and analysis

I. Introduction

Pesticides are widely used in agriculture to protect crops and seeds and may have contributed to improvement in society health and economy. At the same time, widespread use of pesticides has led to serious harm on the environment and human health [1]. With the increasing demand for a high quality agricultural products, new quality and safety control devices are being investigated. Because pesticides damaging effects are invisible and cannot be directly warned by visible observation or simple testing, pesticides estimation in soil or in foods prior to their consumption, requires complex techniques and remains very challenging [2].

A number of analytical methods, including mass spectroscopy gas and liquid chromatography gas chromatography–mass spectrometry (GC-MS), have been reported to detect various pesticides contamination in foods and these methods are very sensitive and reliable [2]. However, these classical analytical approaches are usually confined to a laboratory environment and require costly, long sample preparation time, solvent wasting, and hazardous samples contact [2] [4]. Additional disadvantages of these methods include the restricted database mapping of pesticides analysis and the possibility of false negatives in the results [5].

Biosensors provides a promising alternative for the detection of pesticides. Biosensors convert the signal produced by the immobilized biological element that detect the analyte into an electrically detectable signal and can be classified from their signal transduction techniques into electrochemical, optical, piezoelectric and mechanical biosensors [6]. Many biosensors designed for pesticides detection are based on the inhibition reaction or catalytic activity of several enzymes after pesticides contact [7]. Electrochemical transducers are usually simple to design, small and affordable making them candidate of choices for portable pesticides detection [6]. For instance, Enzyme-Linked ImmunoSorbent Assays (ELISA) have grown rapidly as tools for pesticide measurement, although still challenged [7]. Since a number of pesticides have a similar mode of action affecting the activity of the same enzyme, most of ELISA based biosensors suffer poor individual pesticide specificity although improper to detect total pesticide content. On the other hand, immunosensors are biosensors that senses specific pesticides using antibodies (Ab) or antigens (Ag) taking advantage of the newest development of Ab technologies, targeted against pesticide molecules. Immunosensors are therefore able to provide concentration-dependent results in a certain range [7][8] . For instance in [9], Triazines were assayed using florescent antibodies (conjugated with with fluoresceine isothiocyanate binding to the fibre surface). After contact with the pesticide Triazines the fluorescence signal decreased since less antibodies were binding to the fibre. The detection limit using this immunosensor was very satisfying (around 0.1 ng/ml) [9]. However, there is a time gap between current status in the field and the most recent created immunosensors [7]. In addition, immunosensors usually requires specific testing procedures and have low reusability capacity without loss of sensitivity for most of them [10][11][12].

Due to the great amount of pesticides currently being used, there is an augmented concern in the investigation and creation of rapid and non-destructive methods for pesticides detection [13]. In the last few years, advanced in optical instruments allowed the residuals of insecticides detection from agricultural samples [5]. Detection of hydrophobic organic pollutants via UV, Raman, and IR spectroscopic methods directly at solid sorbent phases are usually reported to be less sensitive than conventional chromatographic analysis, but permit on-site pollution measurements [4].

Near Infrared spectroscopy (NIR) is a well described method to assess the composition and quality of products in the food industry, since it has the capability to analyze organic substances rapidly and cost-effectively, although suffering of low spectral resolution for samples in aqueous solutions due to strong water infrared absorption. As an example, a model for the quality control of herbicide Diuron in intact olives with 85.9% of accuracy using reflectance NIR spectroscopy is presented in [14]. Peppers are a frequent object of food safety alerts in various member states of the European Union since they frequently contain unauthorised pesticide residues. Near Infrared Reflectance Spectroscopy (NIRS) for the measurement of pesticide residues in peppers using commercially available spectrophotometers and demonstrating satisfying results is proposed in [15]. Spectral information in the ranges 1644–1772 and 2014–2607 nm without baseline correction and Partial Least Square (PLS) model interpretation were used to detect Buprofezin, Diuron and Daminozide without any sample pre-treatment and sample destruction in [16].

Diuron determination in pesticide formulations was also analyzed after its extraction with acetonitrile and subsequent transmittance NIR measurements (2021 and 2047 nm). Diuron limit of detection reached 0.013 $mg.g^{-1}$ with this methodology which was 10 times higher than that the results obtained by Liquid Chromatography (LC), making NIR vibrational method appropriate for the quality control of pesticide commercial formulations [17]. Fourier transform near infrared (FT-NIR) spectroscopy is also of value for the determination of pesticides in agrochemicals. Following previous extraction of the active principles and transmission measurements were performed on Chlorsulfuron, Metamitron, Iprodione, Pirimicarb, Procymidone and Tricyclazole, leading to detection values limits ranging from 0.004 to 0.17 $mg.g^{-1}$, 10 times faster than chromatography analysis [18]. Chlopyrifos residue detection in white radish, based on NIR spectroscopy and PLS regression is proposed in [20]. PLS was mainly permitted the determination of the optimum wave number range.

Field portable NIR spectrometer (from 360 to 1690 nm) was able to determine nutrient composition of beef feedlot manure in [19]. On the basis of analysis of dried mannure samples, the field-portable NIR spectrometer allowed fast determination of Carbon, Nitrates, and several other parameters. [19]. Field portable pesticides detectors, based on NIR spectrometry could be therefore considered for pesticides detection using a similar procedure.

Infrared (IR) spectroscopy provides a rapid, low cost and highly reproducible diagnostic screening tool. IR spectroscopy is currently employed for soil surveillance systems, crops health and water quality assessment. [22]. For instance, soil absorption over the Visible/Near-InfraRed (Vis/NIR) wavelength regions (350–2500 nm) is mostly associated with (1) the vibrational energy transitions of the dominant molecular bonds of Fe-oxides (which have absorptions over the visible (350–780 nm) and short-wave NIR (780–1100 nm) spectral regions), (2) clay minerals (which have absorption over the long-wave NIR (1100–2500 nm) regions), (3) water (which has strong absorption features over Vis/NIR regions, most visibly near 1400 and 1900 nm), and (4) organic matter (which has distinct absorption features over the Vis/NIR, due to the various complex chemical bonds) [21]. Under certain conditions, such as very high concentration in soil, some transition elements (including Ni, Cu, Co) may also exhibit absorption features in the Vis/NIR spectral regions [21], permitting direct soil characterization and estimation of pesticides utilization in fields. A Vis/NIR mobile soil sensor was developed in [24] composed by optical unit to detect soil extractable phosphorous (305 and 1711 nm in reflectance mode).

Vis/NIR spectroscopy also permits pesticides and other food contaminants detection. It may be particularly suited for free space measurement and field studies. Internal and external pesticides damage detection of various fruits in Korea and Japan were detected using non damaging methods, such as Vis/NIR Spectroscopy [23].

Many aromatic pesticides are either naturally fluorescent or photodegrade into fluorescent byproducts and are hence suited for fluorescent spectroscopy detection [25]. For example, Polycyclic Aromatic Hydrocarbons (PAHs), pesticides are naturally fluorescent in aqueous solutions and allows for trace elements detection without previous pesticides concentration procedures [25]. Portable fluorometers are now available on market in a single portative device and with fiber-optic probes that permit remote observations [25].

Progress in Raman spectroscopes and in embedded computation equipment have enabled Raman spectroscopy to be used as an analytical tool for both solid samples and aqueous solutions, offering information permitting to determine the internal content in samples [2]. Because Raman spectrum of compound can furnish narrow and highly resolved bands it contains more complete vibrational information than IR spectrum. It may not require stabilizing materials and needs no chemical or mechanical pretreatment and allows nondestructive extraction of physical information [2][5].

Raman spectroscopic techniques mostly gathers dispersive Raman spectroscopy, Fourier transform Raman spectroscopy and Surface Enhanced Raman Spectroscopy (SERS) [2]. Because conventional Raman spectroscopy is limited to a small scattering cross section and requires large amount of specimen and strong incident light, the employment of SERS greatly enhances the sensitivity of the conventional Raman spectroscopy and offers more elevated measurement speed and sensitivity [5].

In food industry, spectroscopy has been satisfactorily used to monitor food quality and safety. For instance Raman spectroscopy was applied to discriminate between transgenic and normal crops in various breeding such as tobacco. Different Raman spectrum were obtained between the transgenic tobacco and the wild type, since for transgenic tobacco, the expression of cinnamyl alcohol dehydrogenase was greatly depleted after cinnamaldehyde lignin incorporation [2]. In addition, Raman spectroscopy was successfully used to distinguish the Brassica napus ‘Drakkar’ from the new genetically modified line [2].

Furthermore, the use of Raman spectroscopy permitted carotenoids content quantification in fruits and vegetables [2]. Other antioxidant quantification such as lycopene could be obtained by NIR-FT-Raman spectroscopy method [2]. FT-Raman spectroscopy method in conjunction with Hierarchical Cluster Analysis (HCA) may accurately assess the energetic value and total carbohydrates, protein, and fat of powdered milk infant formulas [2].

Raman spectroscopic techniques are not only applied in quality control but also in safety control of various beverages, most specifically for microorganisms contamination and adulterants adjunction. The identification of oil adulteration is of great importance from both market and health perspectives in the olive oil industry. Unsaturation of oil Free Fatty Acids (FFA) and total degree of unsaturation could be estimated using spectroscopy measures [2]. Since Raman spectroscopy has been successfully applied to organic compounds detection in food and beverage, its employment for pesticides detection is particularly adequate. Most particularly identification and detection of large family of sulfur-containing pesticide residues at various fruit peels was performed utilizing the shell thickness-dependent Raman enhancement of silver-coated gold nanoparticles [26].

Transmittance spectroscopy is particularly suited for free space measurements without sample preparation and may be applied to pesticides detection. For example, using a transmittance spectroscopy (in the 550 and 980 nm region), insect infested cherries within a tart cherry fruit were detected with accuracy varying from 82% to 87% [27].

Data clustering analysis following spectroscopy data is often required to distinguish food contaminants. Spectroscopy such as SERS coupled with clustering analysis has been shown to enable the trace-level detection of various pesticides [28]. For instance, cluster analysis, following Wavelength Dispersive X Rays Fluorescence Spectroscopy may permit classification of black tea and green tea from tea mineral elements [29]. Clustering algorithms often requires variable fitting or selection methods. Most commonly employed methods are: Stepwise Regression Analysis, Uninformative Variable Elimination, Interval Partial Least Squares (IPLS) regression, Clonal Selection Feature Selection algorithm [13]. As an example improving PLS regression models, used in spectrum data post-processing, may hence result in more specific database inquiries and sample chemical identification.

In this paper, we studied the spectral characteristic of pesticides contamination using Vis-NIR reflectance spectroscopy. Since there are several thousand of different active pesticide molecules reported [30][31], current pesticides detection is limited to few types of pesticides chemical and does not ascertain pesticides free products. We worked from another perspective by comparing the spectral information obtained from pesticides free and pesticides contaminated foods, irrespective of the pesticide types. We searched for particular traces in the spectroscopy spectrum that could be characteristic of pesticides contamination. Mostly two cases could be found: (1) the pesticides grown foods spectra contains additional traces which could be related with pesticides own spectral characteristics or modified endogenous food proteins [32][34], (2) oppositely the absence of spectral components in particular wavelength in pesticides contaminated foods compared to organic or totally natural foods (grown without pesticides addition) may also be used as a spectral indicator of food purity since certain food proteins may not be expressed when pesticides are utilized [35][38].

Further database characterization of these specific spectral components may permit chemical characterization and possibly lead to the creation of a new biomarker for pesticides detection.

Finally, algorithm implementation inside a portative device with an embedded spectrometer, as depicted in Figure 1, permits user centered device for pesticide estimation. For easier user data reading, a wireless communication device (such as WIFI module) is integrated in the embedded system for user's smartphone communication. A specific smartphone application is created for embedded spectrometer results monitoring. To diminish the costs of the overall device, sunlight is used as spectroscopic light source, limiting device utilization in bright areas.

Our document will be organized into 3 main sections: first, the methodology of our experiment will be introduced with the devices used, then, the Vis-NIR spectroscopy results are reported and analyzed, finally a conclusion is drawn with possible future work direction propositions.

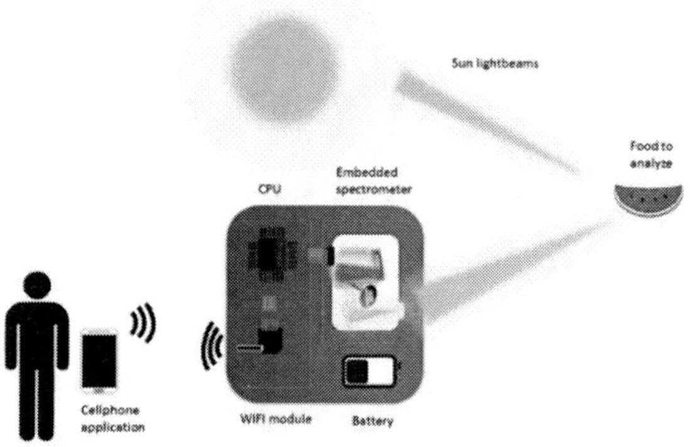

Figure 1. User centric based device for food pesticides monitoring

II. METHODS

Measurements detailed information and equipment used are presented in this Section.

A. *Food samples variety*

TABLE I. VEGETABLE TYPES AND VARIETIES USED FOR THE EXERIMENT

Food Variety (botanical name)	Food suppliers			
	Market gardener (pesticides free)	**Organic shop**	**Supermarket 1**	**Supermarket 2**
Poataoes	*Solanum tuberosum 'Charlotte' (yellow), Solanum tuberosum 'Desiree' (red),*	*Solanum tuberosum 'Charlotte' (yellow)*	*'Cherie'*	*'Cherie'*
Zucchini	*Cucurbita moschata, Cucurbita pepo 'De Nice à fruit ronds'*	*Cucurbita pepo 'Verte non coureuse'*	*Cucurbita pepo 'Verte non coureuse'*	*Cucurbita pepo 'Verte non coureuse'*
Tomatoes	*Lycopersicon escubentum*	*Lycopersicon escubentum, Solanum lycopersicum*	*Lycopersicon escubentum Lycopersicon esculentum*	*Lycopersicon escubentum Lycopersicon esculentum*

We tested 3 different food categories: tomatoes, zucchini and potatoes. The precise variety of vegetable tested is reported in Table I. Food were bought directly from (1) a market gardener that did not used any pesticides or chemical contaminant, (2) an organic store and from 2 famous French supermarket brands, where we assumed that plants were grown using pesticides ((3) and (4)). Although several pesticides are contained in the vegetable peel, we decided to perform the measure on the decorticated vegetable to avoid peel color bias. Each vegetable was tested in 3 different areas.

B. *Test system description:*

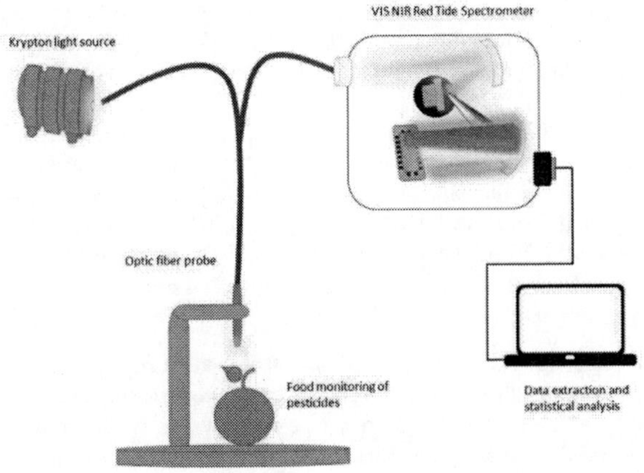

Figure 2. Test bench diagram used for Vis-NIR spectroscopy measurements in various vegetables

Reflectance spectroscopy measures were performed using the test bench described in Figure 2. We used the Ocean Optics kit including the ECOVIS Krypton Lightsource, the USB-650 Red Tide Spectrometer (preconfigured in the 350-1000 nm wavelength range), a 200 um Bifurcated Fiber (Vis-NIR) and the OceanView software. The results were then extracted and manipulated with Matlab software. The distance between the bifurcated fiber and the sample to measure was fixed to 5mm, and the reflectance robe was positioned at an angle of 90° to the flat surface of the sample to analyze.

C. *Data analysis:*

The data were analyzed using Matlab software. First, correction of the light intensity was performed by dividing each sample with its respective Area Under Curve value. Then, we computed the mean value associated with one food type and origin. Mean values of the pesticides free foods spectral data were used to create filters in order to highlight the particular wavelength associated with food pesticides addition.

III. RESULTS

Tomatoes spectroscopy measures from different supplier's origin are presented in Figure 3, after division by their respective Area Under Curve, to remove the measures light intensity drift. Pesticides free tomatoes spectral data mean value is reported in thick blue line for initial comparison. Each subfigure represents the spectral measurements realized on tomatoes from a market gardener that did not used any pesticides or chemical contaminant (top left subfigure), an organic store (top right subfigure) and from 2 famous French supermarket brands, where we assumed that plants were grown using pesticides (bottom left and bottom right subfigures). For each different tomatoes supplier, measures were performed on several vegetable samples to decrease the samples intervariability bias and were reported in different color thin lines in each subfigure. As an example, the top right subfigure of Figure 4 green thin line outlines the relative light intensity of the first pesticide free tomato analyzed and the magenta thin lines outlines the relative light intensity of the third pesticide free tomatoes analyzed.

Figure 4 and Figure 5 depict the spectral measures associated with zucchini and potatoes from different food supplier's origin respectively. For easier data interpretation, light intensity drift is removed by similar integral division. The mean relative light intensity values of the pesticides free zucchini and potatoes are both reported in blue thick lines in each figure. Similarly to the previous figure results, subfigures describe the spectral measurements associated with the 4 different vegetables origin (from pesticide free market gardener, organic store, supermarket 1 and supermarket 2). In each subfigure, the colored thin lines, outline the relative light intensity associated with a specific vegetable sample but from the same supplier origin.

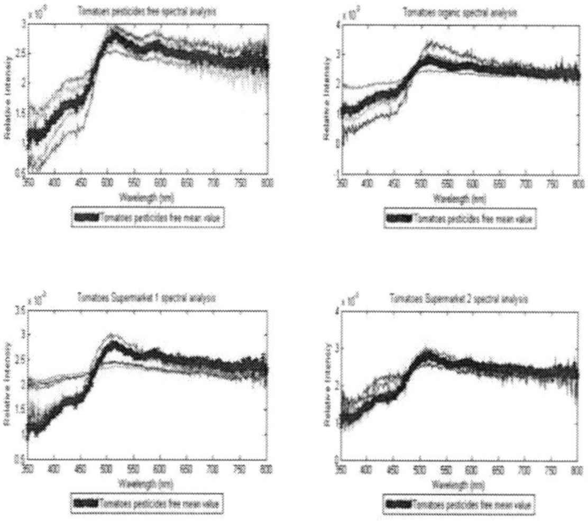

Figure 3. Tomatoes spectral analysis comparison. The samples data are displayed by the colored thin lines and the mean value (only associated with the pesticides free spectrum) is depicted with the thick blue line.

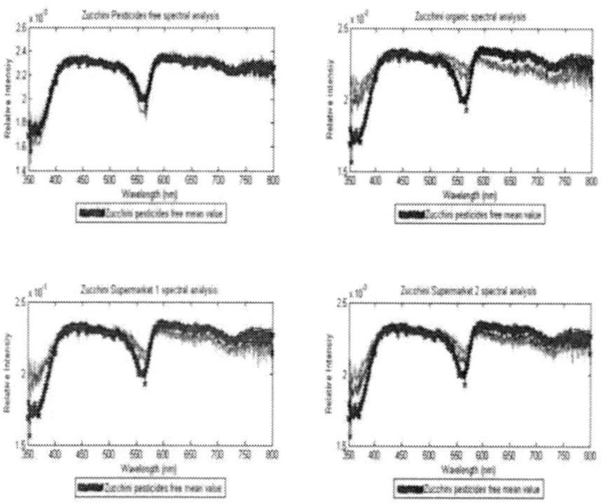

Figure 4. Zucchini spectral data comparison. The sample data are displayed by the colored thin lines and the mean value (only associated with the pesticides free spectrum) is depicted with the thick blue line.

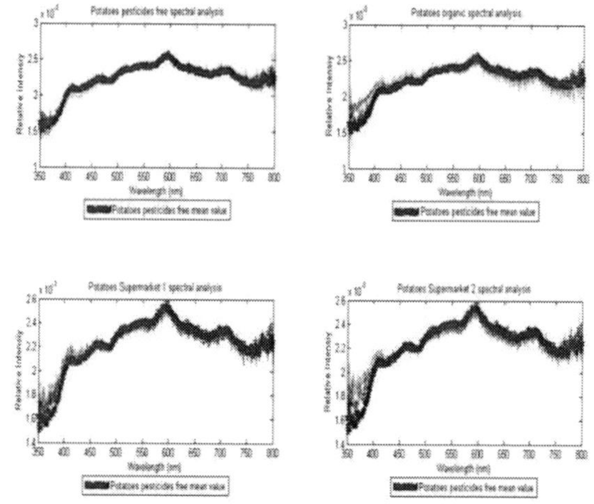

Figure 5. Potatoes spectral data comparison. The sample data are displayed by the colored thin lines and the mean value (only associated with the pesticides free spectrum) is depicted with the thick blue line.

Spectral filtration of mean spectral data from organic shop (blue line), supermarket 1 (green line) and supermarker 2 (red line) with tomatoes, zucchini and potatoes pesticides free mean value are respectively presented in Figure 6, Figure 7 and in Figure 8.

Figure 6 shows that spectral relative intensity in the 350 nm – 400 nm region is particularly characteristic of the tomatoes added chemicals. Other spectral rays (435 nm, 587 nm, 672 nm, 781nm, 791 nm, etc.) deserve extended analysis and database characterization.

Although characterization of food additives or pesticides contaminants for zucchini seems straightforward with two large peaks at 374 nm and 570 nm compared to pesticides free zucchini (Figure 7), the analysis may be more complex. In fact, as presented in Table I, the zucchini variety of the organic shop, supermarket 1 and supermarket 2 (*Cucurbita pepo 'Verte non coureuse'*) is not exactly the same as the one proposed by the pesticide free market gardener (*Cucurbita moschata* and *Cucurbita pepo 'De Nice à fruit ronds')*. Modification in chromophore molecules between these two varieties of zucchini may explain the large results variation. For more conclusive analysis, data obtained from organic zucchini should be used for spectral filter construction, although we further noted that in these wavelength areas, data obtained from organic stores also differ from the ones associated from the two supermarkets. Of particular interest seems to be the spectral rays of 715 nm, 774 nm, 450 - 456 nm area and need deeper investigation.

Spectral filtration of mean spectral data from organic shop (blue line), supermarket 1 (green line) and supermarket 2 (red line) with potatoes pesticides free mean value is described in Figure 8. Except in the 350 nm - 450 nm region, spectral data obtained from the two supermarkets (green and red curves) seems to be closer to the pesticide free spectrum. Several explanations may exist. Like for zucchini, not the same potato varieties were compared, explaining the discrepancies between results. A second explanation is the presence of specific food additional substances, possibly pollutants, in organic food compared to supermarket ones (organic foods are not entirely devoid of pesticides [39]).

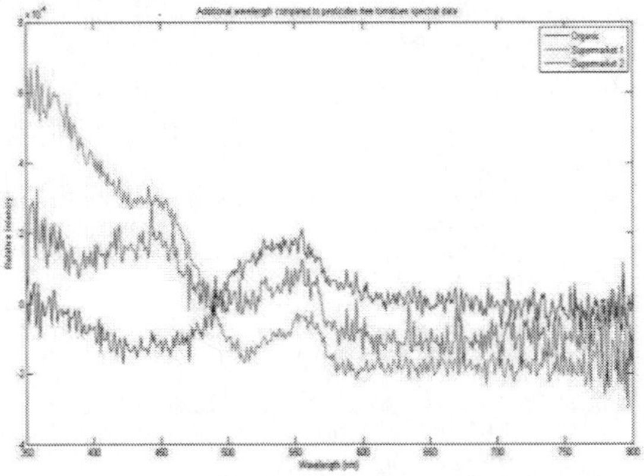

Figure 6. Additional relative light intensity compared to pesticides free tomatoes spectral data

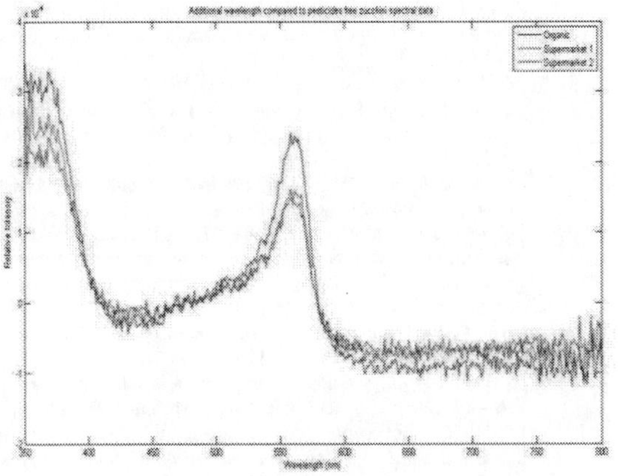

Figure 7. Additional relative light intensity compared to pesticides free zucchini spectral data

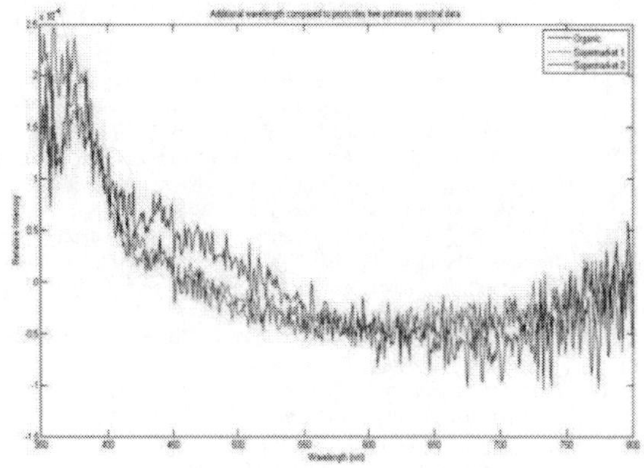

Figure 8. Additional relative light intensity compared to pesticides free potatoes spectral data

IV. CONCLUSION AND FUTURE WORK

Although insufficiently characterized and currently incomplete, spectroscopic analysis of food in the Vis-NIR wavelength range, seems to permit food quality estimation. We propose an innovative method based on Vis-NIR spectroscopy for detecting food contaminants using spectral filters constructed from pesticides free food samples data. Our methodology choices was mainly dictated by the countless number of food contaminants, which are currently limiting the detection to only a restricted number of well-known contaminants spectrum traces for filters creation. In contrast we used the Vis-NIR spectral trace of pesticides free foods for filter creation.

From early conclusion, our methods seems promising and easy to implement. However very meticulous data should be obtained first for each pesticides free food variety studied. Modification of the internal food coloration including food maturity levels, seeds number, etc. can lead to different light intensity spectral analysis, generating important unpredictability in the reference spectral data.

Once extracted the particular wavelength associated with food pollutants, such as pesticides, database search may further permit pollutants chemical characterization.

Moreover, because of the access difficulties to many varieties of pesticides free grown foods, organic foods may be used in first approximation although not always devoid of contaminants.

Finally, the implementation of such algorithm in an embedded platform with a microspectrometer module may allow device user estimation of foods chemical contaminants.

REFERENCES

[1] D. Pimentel, "Environmental and economic costs of the application of pesticides primarily in the United States," *Environment, development and sustainability*, vol. 7, pp. 229-252, 2005.

[2] D. Yang and Y. Ying, "Applications of Raman spectroscopy in agricultural products and food analysis: A review," *Applied Spectroscopy Reviews*, vol. 46, pp. 539-560, 2011.

[3] D. Lee, S. Lee, *et al.*, "Quantitative analysis of methyl parathion pesticides in a polydimethylsiloxane microfluidic channel using confocal surface-enhanced Raman spectroscopy," *Applied spectroscopy*, vol. 60, pp. 373-377, 2006.

[4] M. Karlowatz, M. Kraft, and B. Mizaikoff, "Simultaneous quantitative determination of benzene, toluene, and xylenes in water using mid-infrared evanescent field spectroscopy," *Analytical chemistry*, vol. 76, pp. 2643-2648, 2004.

[5] K. Wong-Ek, *et al.*, "Portable surface-enhanced Raman spectroscopy for insecticide detection using silver nanorod film fabricated by magnetron sputtering," in *SPIE BiOS*, 2011, pp. 791108-791108-11.

[6] A. Sassolas, B. Prieto-Simón, and J.-L.Marty, "Biosensors for Pesticide Detection: New Trends," *American Journal of Analytical Chemistry*, pp. 210-232, 2012.

[7] X. Jiang, *et al.*, "Immunosensors for detection of pesticide residues," *Biosensors and Bioelectronics*, vol. 23, pp. 1577-1587, 2008.

[8] C. R. Suri, M. Raje, and G. C. Varshney, "Immunosensors for pesticide analysis: antibody production and sensor development," *Critical reviews in biotechnology*, vol. 22, pp. 15-32, 2002.

[9] F. Bier, W. Stöcklein, M. Böcher, U. Bilitewski, and R. Schmid, "Use of a fibre optic immunosensor for the detection of pesticides," *Sensors and Actuators B: Chemical*, vol. 7, pp. 509-512, 1992.

[10] M.-I. Baraton, *Sensors for Environment, Health and Security: Advanced Materials and Technologies*: Springer Science & Business Media, 2008.

[11] M. Ferrari, M. Ozkan, and M. Heller, *BioMEMS and Biomedical Nanotechnology: Volume II: Micro/Nano Technologies for Genomics and Proteomics* vol. 2: Springer Science & Business Media, 2007.

[12] O. Tigli, *Novel SAW devices in CMOS for biosensor applications: design, modeling, fabrication and characterization*: ProQuest, 2007.

[13] L. Xue, J. Cai, J. Li, and M. Liu, "Application of particle swarm optimization (PSO) algorithm to determine dichlorvos residue on the surface of navel orange with Vis-NIR spectroscopy," *Procedia Engineering*, vol. 29, pp. 4124-4128, 2012.

[14] L. Salguero-Chaparro, A. J. Gaitán-Jurado, V. Ortiz-Somovilla, and F. Peña-Rodríguez, "Feasibility of using NIR spectroscopy to detect herbicide residues in intact olives," *Food control*, vol. 30, pp. 504-509, 2013.

[15] M. T. Sánchez, K. Flores-Rojas, J. E. Guerrero, A. Garrido-Varo, and D. Pérez-Marín, "Measurement of pesticide residues in peppers by near-infrared reflectance spectroscopy," *Pest management science*, vol. 66, pp. 580-586, 2010.

[16] S. Armenta, S. Garrigues, and M. de la Guardia, "Partial least squares-near infrared determination of pesticides in commercial formulations," *Vibrational Spectroscopy*, vol. 44, pp. 273-278, 2007.

[17] J. Moros, S. Armenta, S. Garrigues, and M. de la Guardia, "Near infrared determination of Diuron in pesticide formulations," *Analytica chimica acta*, vol. 543, pp. 124-129, 2005.

[18] J. Moros, S. Armenta, S. Garrigues, and M. de la Guardia, "Univariate near infrared methods for determination of pesticides in agrochemicals," *Analytica chimica acta*, vol. 579, pp. 17-24, 2006.

[19] D. Malley, C. McClure, P. Martin, K. Buckley, and W. McCaughey, "Compositional analysis of cattle manure during composting using a field-portable near-infrared spectrometer," *Communications in Soil Science and Plant Analysis*, vol. 36, pp. 455-475, 2005.

[20] Y. Zhou, B. Xiang, Z. Wang, and C. Chen, "Determination of chlorpyrifos residue by near-infrared spectroscopy in white radish based on interval partial least square (iPLS) model," *Analytical Letters*, vol. 42, pp. 1518-1526, 2009.

[21] T. Shi, Y. Chen, Y. Liu, and G. Wu, "Visible and near-infrared reflectance spectroscopy—An alternative for monitoring soil contamination by heavy metals," *Journal of hazardous materials*, vol. 265, pp. 166-176, 2014.

[22] K. D. Shepherd and M. G. Walsh, "Infrared spectroscopy—enabling an evidence-based diagnostic surveillance approach to agricultural and environmental management in developing countries," *Journal of Near Infrared Spectroscopy*, vol. 15, pp. 1-19, 2007.

[23] S.-H. Noh and K.-H. Choi, "Nondestructive quality evaluation technology for fruits and vegetables," in *International Seminar on Enhancing Export Competitiveness of Asian Fruits, Bangkok, Thailand*, pp. 1-15, 2006.

[24] M. Maleki, A. Mouazen, H. Ramon, and J. De Baerdemaeker, "Optimisation of soil VIS–NIR sensor-based variable rate application system of soil phosphorus," *Soil and Tillage Research*, vol. 94, pp. 239-250, 2007.

[25] R. D. JiJi, G. A. Cooper, and K. S. Booksh, "Excitation-emission matrix fluorescence based determination of carbamate pesticides and polycyclic aromatic hydrocarbons," *Analytica Chimica Acta*, vol. 397, pp. 61-72, 1999.

[26] B. Liu, *et al.*, "Shell thickness-dependent Raman enhancement for rapid identification and detection of pesticide residues at fruit peels," *Analytical chemistry*, vol. 84, pp. 255-261, 2011.

[27] J. Xing and D. Guyer, "Detecting internal insect infestation in tart cherry using transmittance spectroscopy," *Postharvest biology and technology*, vol. 49, pp. 411-416, 2008.

[28] B. Saute, R. Premasiri, L. Ziegler, and R. Narayanan, "Gold nanorods as surface enhanced Raman spectroscopy substrates for sensitive and selective detection of ultra-low levels of dithiocarbamate pesticides," *Analyst*, vol. 137, pp. 5082-5087, 2012.

[29] G. Chunhui, Z. Guoqiang, G. Liangquan, L. Jun, and W. Ziqiang, "Determination of trace elements in tea by wavelength dispersive X-ray fluorescence spectroscopy," *Nuclear Techniques*, vol. 36, 2013.

[30] L. R. Goldman, "Managing pesticide chronic health risks: US policies," *Journal of agromedicine*, vol. 12, pp. 67-75, 2007.

[31] C. f. D. C. a. Prevention. (2013). *CDC - Pesticide Illness & Injury Surveillance - NIOSH Workplace Safety and Health Topic*.

[32] S. Parvez and S. Raisuddin, "Protein carbonyls: novel biomarkers of exposure to oxidative stress-inducing pesticides in freshwater fish Channa punctata (Bloch)," *Environmental Toxicology and Pharmacology*, vol. 20, pp. 112-117, 2005.

[33] J. Dorts, *et al.*, "Oxidative stress, protein carbonylation and heat shock proteins in the black tiger shrimp, Penaeus monodon, following exposure to endosulfan and deltamethrin," *Environmental toxicology and pharmacology*, vol. 28, pp. 302-310, 2009.

[34] J. J. Fortunato, *et al.*, "Malathion-induced oxidative stress in rat brain regions," *Neurochemical research*, vol. 31, pp. 671-678, 2006.

[35] S. B. Ceyhun, *et al.*, "Deltamethrin attenuates antioxidant defense system and induces the expression of heat shock protein 70 in rainbow trout," *Comparative Biochemistry and Physiology Part C: Toxicology & Pharmacology*, vol. 152, pp. 215-223, 2010.

[36] R. M. Johnson, J. D. Evans, G. E. Robinson, and M. R. Berenbaum, "Changes in transcript abundance relating to colony collapse disorder in honey bees (Apis mellifera)," *Proceedings of the National Academy of Sciences*, vol. 106, pp. 14790-14795, 2009.

[37] H. T. Hogberg, A. Kinsner-Ovaskainen, T. Hartung, S. Coecke, and A. K. Bal-Price, "Gene expression as a sensitive endpoint to evaluate cell differentiation and maturation of the developing central nervous system in primary cultures of rat cerebellar granule cells (CGCs) exposed to pesticides," *Toxicology and applied pharmacology*, vol. 235, pp. 268-286, 2009.

[38] M. Collotta, P. Bertazzi, and V. Bollati, "Epigenetics and pesticides," *Toxicology*, vol. 307, pp. 35-41, 2013.

[39] B. P. Baker, C. M. Benbrook, E. G. III, and K. L. Benbrook, "Pesticide residues in conventional, integrated pest management (IPM)-grown and organic foods: insights from three US data sets," *Food Additives & Contaminants*, vol. 19, pp. 427-446, 2002.

User Blood and Organs Pesticides Concentration Estimation System Based on Two Compartments Parmacokinetic Models

Umberto Cerasani
CERAGOS Electronics and Nature
Sophia Antipolis, France
Email:cerasani@ceragos.org

Dominique Bedra
CERAGOS Electronics and Nature
Sophia Antipolis, France

***Abstract*—Pesticides are omnipresent in foods and drinks and their toxic effects are becoming evident, as well as their correlation with many diseases. Pesticides intoxication estimation could lead to lifestyle modification before certain disease symptoms occurrence. User centered application for pesticides blood and tissues concentration is proposed in this document, based on location, profession, mean food consumption and personal lifestyle indications. Three different mathematical PBPK models are used to create such system and parametrized from user personal data. User blood and tissues concentration of organophosphates per day or per year are speculated and indicated to the user.**

***Keywords*—Mathematical models; Pesticides; Pharmacokinetic modeling; user centerd application**

I. Introduction

The Food and Agriculture Organization (FAO) defines a pesticide as: "any substance or mixture intended for preventing, destroying or controlling any pest, including vectors of human or animal disease, unwanted species of plants or animals causing harm during or otherwise interfering with the production, processing, storage or marketing of food [...]" [1].

In 2006 and 2007, approximately 2.4 billion kilograms of pesticides were utilized in the United States, comprising mainly herbicides (40%), followed by insecticides (17%) and fungicides (10%). The same year, more than 1,055 active ingredients were registered as pesticides [1][2].

Many pesticides can be grouped into chemical families and target organism families. Plant-derived pesticides mainly include the pyrethroids, rotenoids, nicotinoids, strychnine and scilliroside. Prominent insecticide families comprising organochlorines, organophosphates, and carbamates. Organochlorine hydrocarbons (such as DDT) could be further classified into dichlorodiphenylethanes, cyclodiene compounds, and other related compounds. Prominent families of herbicides include phenoxy and benzoic acid herbicides, triazines, ureas, and Chloroacetanilides [3].

It is estimated that over 98% of sprayed insecticides and 95% of herbicides undergoes pesticide drift since air suspended pesticides are carried out to unwanted areas [4][6]. Pesticides are one main cause of water pollution because most of currently used pesticides are Persistent Organic Pollutants (POP) and contribute to long lasting soil contamination [7]. Their toxicities vary greatly, as well as their persistence and potential to bio-accumulate [8][11].

In certain endemic areas, pesticides are used to kill mosquitoes that can transmit potentially deadly diseases like Malaria and can protect animals from deadly parasites [2][12]. Pesticides therefore provide variety of benefits in agriculture, although there are multiple undesirable and unwanted effects of pesticide usage that are now becoming apparent. In industrialized world, most of the pesticides contamination occurs in long term and low level exposure except for few directly exposed agricultural or manufacturing workers who suffer long-term high-level exposure or less frequently acute poisoning, whereas in the countries of the developing world, the situation is almost reversed [13].

Pesticides health effects, which can be acute or delayed, are difficult to characterize since they interact with a plethora of enzymes, proteins, receptors and transcription factors [14].

Countless studies demonstrate the detrimental impact of pesticides in human health. Many organophosphate pesticides are potent nerve agents, functioning by inhibiting the action of acetylcholinesterase (AChE) in nerve cells and have been linked to increased Parkinson's disease occurrence and may explain increased autism frequency rate in developed countries [15][17][18]. Several pesticides have been documented to affect the endocrine system from synthesis to hormone receptor binding, acting as Endocrine Disrupting Chemicals (EDC) [14]. Pesticides such as atrazine have hazardous impact on reproductive system and fetus development and have been shown to emasculate three-quarters of exposed male frogs [19][21]. Furthermore a growing number of epidemiological and molecular studies provide substantial evidence that the pesticides are associated with increased cancer risk [22]. Analyzes presented in [23] provide additional evidence for a causative relation between Pendimethalin, Dieldrin, and Parathion use and lung cancer risk. Pesticides are recognized carcinogenic for several cancers including prostate cancer, non-Hodgkin lymphoma, leukemia, multiple myeloma, and breast cancer [24]. Monitoring or estimating blood and tissues pesticides levels is hence of capital importance to prevent or cure an important number of prevalent diseases.

Quantitative Structure Activity Relationships (QSARs), are mathematical models, mostly based on Multiple Linear Regression or Partial Least Square algorithms, that attempt to relate the structure-derived features of a compound to its biological or physicochemical activity [25][26]. Although efficiently assessing acute toxicity risk linked to a chemical, chronic toxicity presents a challenge for QSAR modelling, which should ideally focus on groups of chemicals with a common mode of action [27].

Physiologically Based Pharmaco-Kinetic (PBPK) models consist of a series of mathematical representations simulating the Absorption, Distribution, Metabolism, and Excretion (ADME) of chemicals that enter the body. PBPK models utilize experimentally accepted physiological and biochemical data to predict concentrations of chemical at target tissues or organs for a wide variety of exposure scenarios [28].

PBPK rather than QSAR models have emerged as satisfactory computational approach supporting quantitative risk assessment of agrochemicals [29]. Rat study based on radiolabeled Oxadiazin and Thiamethoxan injection showed that one compartment PBPK model fits best [30]. Population Pharmacokinetic Analysis of Paraquat in Mice Following a Single Paraquat Oral Dose was performed in [31]. Cumulative risk assessment for organophosphate pesticide using PBPK model is reported in [32]. PBPK modeling was used to predict the total dose of Chlorpyrifos received by an individual from urinary biomarker measurements [33]. Since Animal studies suggest that Atrazine overexposure causes Parkinson Disease like dopaminergic toxicities, new PBPK models of Atrazine rodents exposure across the lifespan have been successfully developed [34]. Because recent exposures of organophosphate pesticides have shifted from multipathways to dietary ingestion only, modification of PBPK model input data is central to correct risk assessment and data validation [35].

In this paper, we aim to construct a system estimating user blood and other tissues pesticides levels following different types of exposure, using a two compartments PBPK model. Based on user location, job and data, a valuation of pesticides blood and tissues levels per year is proposed and near future pesticides body internal levels could be extrapolated.

The first section of this document presents the general principle of the user based system developed, the second section introduces the theoretical basis of our model construction, mostly based on drugs pharmacokinetic mathematical models. The following section describes the corresponding results obtained from experimentally defined parameters. A final discussion concludes this paper, presenting the theoretical benefits and limitation of this proposed modeling work.

II. USER CENTERED SYSTEM OF INFORMATION

Estimating blood and other tissue pesticides is very challenging, partial, limited to a few compounds and most of the time highly speculative or inexact. We aimed to create an innovative program based on a few samples.

User location once correlated to pesticides estimation maps per countries area which are available for certain regions, allowed to assess user exposure levels to water and air pesticides. The amount of food consumed per week and the quality of it is also a capital information helping to determine personal user pesticides exposure. We further develop 3 different PBPK models which were selected from user profession and location and corresponding to (1) low levels long lasting exposure (all population group), (2) middle to high levels long lasting exposure (pesticides manufacturer, user close to large agricultural fields, etc.), (3) very elevated models of exposure in a short time (pesticides poisoning corresponding to farmer pesticides dissemination periods, etc.). Finally, user lifestyle general data were also taken into consideration, such as the amount of sport per week since sweating may help in pesticides elimination for instance.

Our program uses these values as parameters which were injected into different mathematical models to finally inform the user of its mean exposure exposition every day and user specific pesticides accumulation per year are speculated.

Two types of user based systems are currently being developed: (1) the first requires user connection to an interactive website, (2) the second system is a smartphone apps, requiring the same user informative procedure and connecting to the same processing center address were computations are made. Then, user pesticides accumulation assessment are reported to the user, associated with general population statistics. Both systems are introduced in Figure 1.

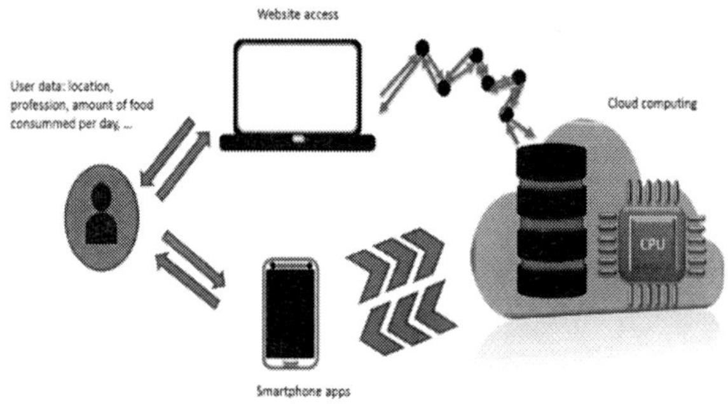

Figure 1. CENTRIC based system for user pesticides estimation

III. METHODOLOGY AND MODEL PARAMETERS

Compartment models theoretical basis are generally described in [36][37][38]. They aim to characterize the dynamics of state variables in various volumes referred as compartments. PBPK drugs studies permit to characterize the dose-concentration-effect/toxicity relationship, evaluates the drug/disease interactions and simulate the drug responses in various organs [39]. Although very complex and multi-compartments models exist for drugs predictive evaluation [40], intervening in drug product development, analysis of pesticides dynamics once introduced in the body are less numerous [35][37][41][43].

The two compartments PBPK model was preferred since single compartment model does not correctly model pesticides accumulation in tissues and because pesticides blood concentration often involves two distinct biological half-live: one associated with rapid plasma removal and the other with long lasting pesticides accumulation in tissues [44]. Obviously, more complex PBPK models could have been used, permitting to more efficiently correlates pesticides accumulation in certain tissues and associated diseases occurrence, but pesticides distribution in tissues is insufficiently characterized in current literature. For instance, our model does not include permanent body pesticides stores which may be the case in real world such as bones or brain accumulation pools.

Various pesticides kinetics experiments, mostly based on rats are reported in Table I, corresponding to the [31][34][45][46] results. Performing interspecies results extrapolation of most of the parameters involved was proven acceptable according to [47] and parameters determined from rats experiments can be directly applied to humans by modifying only the body weight.

Since the pesticides containing the organophosphates Parathion and Diazinon individuate the parameters needed for the two compartment PBPK model adaptation to pesticides, we chose to restrict our models to organophosphates Parathion and Diazinon only. The conclusion for other pesticides may vary greatly since the molecules involved could be totally different as their metabolism in the human body. Besides, in the result section we report pesticides models conclusions only based on Parathion and Diazinon pesticides dynamics and much diverse results may be obtained from different pesticides type.

The two compartments PBPK model we used in described in Figure 2, where K_a represents the absorption rate, K_e the elimination rate, K_c and K_d the inter-compartment exchange rate and K_m the metabolic rate of the Peripheral Compartment (PC). We neglected K_m in the first place although specific metabolic models such as Michaelis Menten could have been used [48][50]. The volume of the Central Compartment (CC) is referred as V_c which includes highly irrigated and poorly storing pesticides organs as well as plasma whereas V_p represents the volume of pesticides internalizing organs.

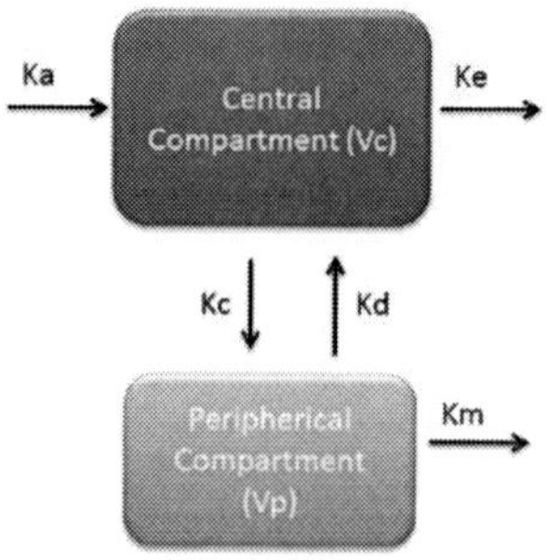

Figure 2. Two compartment pharmacokinetic model used for tissue drug repartition and evolution

A. *Mathematical PBPK models of intravenous injection:*

According to the two compartments PBPK model, we suppose that the toxins concentration ($C_c(t)$) in the Central Compartment (CC) is described by (1):

$$C_c(t) = Ae^{-\alpha t} + Be^{-\beta t} \qquad (1)$$

where $Ae^{-\alpha t}$ models the distribution phase of the organophosphates from the CC to the PC or the amount of organophosphates directly excreted. In contrast $Be^{-\beta t}$ models the elimination phase where both CC and PC excrete the pesticides accumulated.

The mathematical expression presented here corresponds to an intravenous injection of the organophosphates without PC metabolic activity ($K_a = 0$ and $K_m = 0$).

Defining $m_c(t)$ the mass of pesticides in the CC and $m_p(t)$ the mass of pesticides in the PC and applying the mass conservation principle, we obtain (2):

$$(S_1)\begin{cases}\frac{dm_c(t)}{dt} = (-K_e - K_C) * m_c(t) + K_d * m_p(t) \\ \frac{dm_p(t)}{dt} = K_c * m_c(t) - K_d * m_p(t)\end{cases} \quad (2)$$
$$\rightarrow \begin{cases} m_c(t) = r * e^{\lambda_1 t} + s * e^{\lambda_2 t} \\ m_p(t) = v * e^{\lambda_1 t} + w * e^{\lambda_2 t}\end{cases}$$

λ_1, λ_2 are the eigenvalues of the matrix $M = \begin{pmatrix} -K_e - K_C & K_d \\ K_c & -K_d \end{pmatrix}$, (r, s, v, w) can be find using the initials conditions, which are identified with experimental measures. Besides, inserting the volume of distribution, permits to relate the toxin mass in the CC with its concentration in this compartment, as described by (3):

$$\frac{m_c(t)}{V_c} = C_c(t)\ with\ V_c = \frac{A+B}{DOSE}$$
$$and\ \frac{m_p(t)}{V_p} = C_p(t)\ with\ V_p = V_c * \frac{K_c}{K_d} \quad (3)$$

where DOSE corresponds to the amount of pesticides injected and was fixed to 5 mg/kg of body weight for the intravenous injection model (bolus model) or to 50 mg/kg of body weight for the oral absorption model, corresponding to the values described in Table I.

The initial conditions are determined from experimental measurements ($m_c(0)$ = DOSE and $m_p(0) = 0$ since the pesticides dose in directly injected in plasma at t = 0) and were injected in the S_1 system yielding (4):

$$\begin{cases} r + s = DOSE \\ \lambda_1 * s + \lambda_2 * r = (-K_e - K_c) * (r+s) \\ v + w = 0 \\ \lambda_1 * v + \lambda_2 * w = K_c * (r+s)\end{cases} \quad (4)$$

Consequently, we obtained:

$$\begin{cases} r = \frac{DOSE * (K_e + K_c + \lambda_2)}{\lambda_2 - \lambda_1} \\ s = -\frac{DOSE * (K_e + K_c + \lambda_1)}{\lambda_2 - \lambda_1} \\ v = -\frac{K_c * (DOSE)}{\lambda_2 - \lambda_1} \\ w = \frac{K_c * (DOSE)}{\lambda_2 - \lambda_1}\end{cases} \quad (5)$$

Since $r = \frac{A}{V_c} = \frac{A*(A+B)}{DOSE}$ $and\ s = \frac{B}{V_c} = \frac{B*(A+B)}{DOSE}$, this leads to the system presented in (6):

$$(S_2)\begin{cases} \frac{A*(A+B)}{DOSE} = \frac{DOSE * (-K_a + K_e + K_c + \lambda_2)}{\lambda_2 - \lambda_1} \\ \frac{B*(A+B)}{DOSE} = -\frac{DOSE * (-K_a + K_e + K_c + \lambda_1)}{\lambda_2 - \lambda_1} \\ \alpha = \lambda_1 \\ \beta = \lambda_2 \end{cases} \quad (6)$$

Solving S_2 permits to extract the value of K_e, K_c, K_d.

Because toxins kinetics are less well characterized than drugs kinetics, toxins body metabolism and excretion are often described by other constants such as biological half-life ($t_{1/2}$), rate of clearance (CL) and excretion rate (K_e). We should hence first find the corresponding (A, B, α, β) from ($t_{1/2}^{fast}$, $t_{1/2}^{slow}$, CL, K_e) before finding the two compartments models parameters (K_c, K_d, …)

The elimination of a drug (or a toxin) in plasma (Central Compartment) has a distribution phase (rapid phase of plasma removal because of elimination and organs accumulation) and a slow phase (only elimination from the CC and PC), two biological half-life are often reported: one attributed to the rapid phase ($t_{1/2}^{fast}$) and one to the slow phase ($t_{1/2}^{slow}$), defining the system of equation (S_3) reported in (7):

$$(S_3)\begin{cases} Ae^{-\alpha t_{1/2}^{fast}} = \frac{A}{2} \rightarrow t_{1/2}^{fast} = \frac{\ln(2)}{\alpha} \\ Be^{-\beta t_{1/2}^{slow}} = \frac{B}{2} \rightarrow t_{1/2}^{slow} = \frac{\ln(2)}{\beta} \\ CL = \frac{DOSE}{\int_0^{\infty}(Ae^{-\alpha t} + Be^{-\beta t})dt} = \frac{DOSE}{\frac{A}{\alpha} + \frac{B}{\beta}} \\ K_e = CL * \frac{DOSE}{A+B}\end{cases} \quad (7)$$

Knowing ($t_{1/2}^{fast}$, $t_{1/2}^{slow}$, CL, K_e) permits to numerically compute (A, B, α, β), using Maple® implementation of the (S_3) system for instance.

B. Mathematical PBPK models of oral pesticides absorption:

Injection of pesticides intravenously only serves theoretical purposes. Pesticides are absorbed by various means and greatly depends on individual location, work and general lifestyle. We chose to model three types of pesticides absorption: (1) one associated with repeated low levels of pesticides absorption (mainly oral through food and drinks contamination) and regarding all population groups, (2) another one associated with constant medium to high levels of pesticides absorption, mostly through skin and lungs and concerning very specialized workers such as pesticides manufacturers and (3) a model associated with high level and short term pesticides absorption corresponding to farmer pesticides exposition during pesticides field deposition.

Accordingly, we modify the intravenous model of pesticides absorption, injecting an input term represented by the function $T_x(t)$. Adding an input function ($T_x(t)$) to the system resulted in a permanent modification of the solution such as expressed in (8):

$$(S_3)\begin{cases}\frac{dm_c(t)}{dt} = (-K_e - K_C) * m_c(t) + K_d * m_p(t) + K_a * T_x(t) \\ \frac{dm_p(t)}{dt} = K_c * m_c(t) - K_d * m_p(t)\end{cases} \quad (8)$$

The solution of this first order differential system of equations ($m_c(t) = r * e^{\lambda_1 t} + s * e^{\lambda_2 t}$ and $m_p(t) = v * e^{\lambda_1 t} + w * e^{\lambda_2 t}$) is similar to the solutions of separated second order differential equations [51][54].

Noticing that the homogeneous solutions of $m_c(t)$ and $m_p(t)$ are similar to homogeneous solution of second order differential equations. Since the two $m_c(t)$ and $m_p(t)$ solutions are mutually independent, the corresponding second order differential equation particular solution can be determined separately.

We first reconstructed the second order homogeneous differential equation generalized form leading to $m_c(t)$ and $m_p(t)$ homogeneous solutions by solving the system presented in (9):

$$(S_4)\begin{cases} a * C_1 * r * \lambda_1^2 + b * C_1 * r * \lambda_1 + c * C_1 * r = 0 \\ a * C_2 * r * \lambda_2^2 + b * C_2 * r * \lambda_2 + c * C_2 * r = 0 \end{cases} \quad (9)$$

Fixing a = 1 to obtain the same number of equations and unknowns, resulted in:

$$\rightarrow \begin{cases} b = -(\lambda_1 + \lambda_2) \\ c = \lambda_1 * \lambda_2 \end{cases} \quad (10)$$

Therefore, the second homogeneous differential equations described in (11), also has $m_c(t) = C_1 * r * e^{\lambda_1 t} + C_2 * s * e^{\lambda_2 t}$ as (homogeneous) solution:

$$\frac{d^2 m_c(t)}{dt^2} + (-\lambda_1 - \lambda_2) * \frac{dm_c(t)}{dt} + (\lambda_1 * \lambda_2) * m_c(t) = 0 \quad (11)$$

Including the input function, leads to the differential equation governing the CC organophosphates pesticides concentration kinetics:

$$\frac{d^2 m_c(t)}{dt^2} + (-\lambda_1 - \lambda_2) * \frac{dm_c(t)}{dt} + (\lambda_1 * \lambda_2) * m_c(t) + K_a * T_x(t) = 0 \quad (12)$$

Finding the particular solution can be achieved using the method of undetermined coefficients such as indicated in [51][53][55]. We used Maple® software to obtain the particular solution for different input function ($T_x(t)$) types.

1) *Constant input function:*

The mathematical description of the generalized solution is presented in (13).

$$m_c(t) = C_1 * r * e^{\lambda_1 t} + C_2 * s * e^{\lambda_2 t} + \frac{K_a * T_x(t)}{\lambda_1 * \lambda_2} \quad (13)$$

It should be notified that the amount of toxins found in plasma after a long period of time exceeding biological half lives is the ratio between the amount of toxins introduced, the absorption rate and the distribution and excretion coefficients.

2) *Decreasing exponential input function:*

This solution is associated with acute single pesticides exposure as it may be the case in various acute pesticides poisoning cases. We chose a decreasing exponential as input function rather than a window function as we consider that withdrawal from pesticides source exposure was gradual rather than suddenly interrupted.

$$m_c(t) = C_1 * r * e^{\lambda_1 t} + C_2 * s * e^{\lambda_2 t} + \frac{K_a * P_0 * e^{-\sigma * t}}{(\lambda_2 + \sigma) * (\lambda_1 + \sigma)} \quad (14)$$

IV. MODELS IMPLEMENTATION RESULTS:

The results presented in this section arise from Maple® software implementation of the two compartments organophosphates PBPK models.

1) *Intravenous injection of organophosphates*

Figure 3 depicts the CC and CP respective concentration of organophosphates. The intravenous injected dose was supposed equal to 0.05 mg/kg of body weight. Human Dianizon plasma clearance (CL) capacity was fixed to 7.58 mg/L, $t_{1/2}^{\alpha}$ to 0.33mg/h, $t_{1/2}^{\beta}$ to 4.70 mg/h.

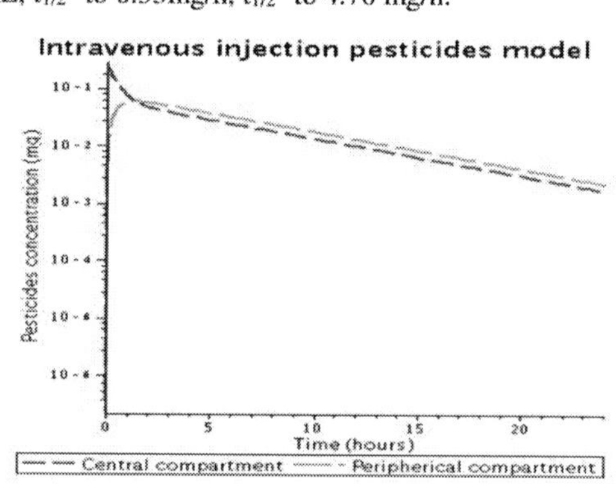

Figure 3. Bolus model of pesticides kinetic in humans

2) *Oral absorption of organophosphates:*

Oral absorption of a single dose of 5mg of organophosphates aimed to analyze the time needed for complete organophosphates clearance of the CC and PC. The absorption rate was based on rat gut measurements and was reported around 1.3 mg/h [45]. The other parameters were maintained similar to the intravenous model and organophosphates concentration in the CC and PC were reported in a normal and semi-log graph (Figure 4).

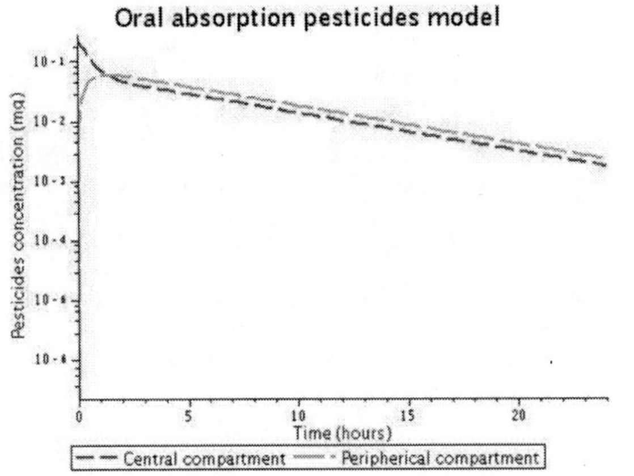

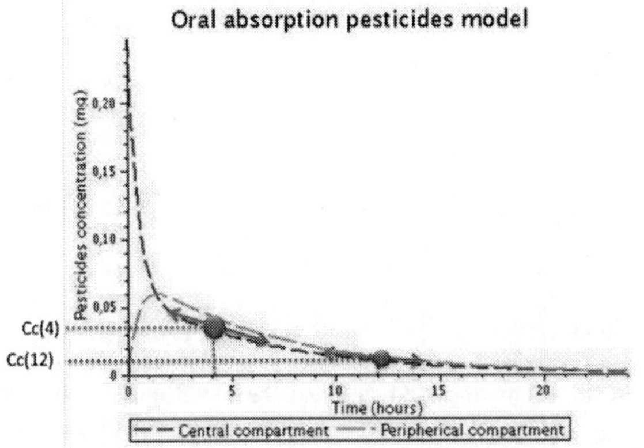

Figure 4. a. Pesticides kinetic following oral absorption in humans (semi-log plot). Figure 4. b. Pesticides kinetic following oral absorption in humans (linear plot)

3) *Constant absorption of organophosphates:*

The third result presented in Figure 5 corresponds to a constant absorption of organophosphates over one day, as it may be the case for individuals living near to highly concentrated pesticides field areas or pesticides manufacturer laboratory employees [56]. The absorption of pesticides is mainly performed through inhalation (K_{al}=15 L/min [57][59]) or through skin absorption (K_{as}=4.81 /cm^2/h [60][61]). We supposed that the dose constantly in contact with population in such areas was around 25 mg/day [62]. Possibly because of excretion mechanisms saturation, the CL rate was decreased (CL = 4.6 mg/L) as well as the fast and slow organophosphate biological half-live in plasma ($t_{1/2}^{\alpha}$ = 0.13 mg/h and $t_{1/2}^{\beta}$ = 1.08 mg/h).

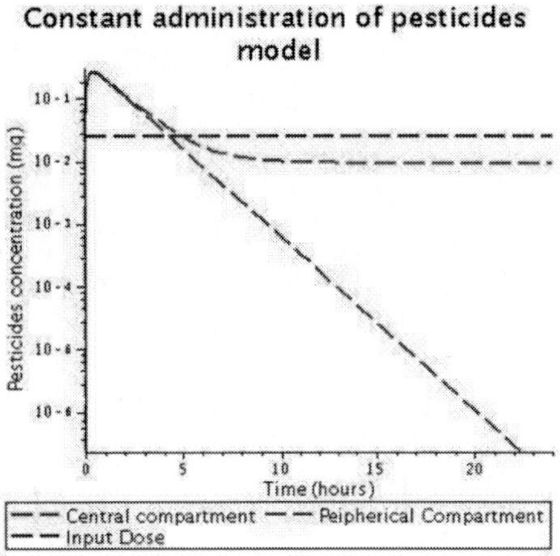

Figure 5. Constant administration of pesticides internal body stores evolution modeling workers involved in specific industries

4) *Acute pesticides intoxication:*

Dose response of organophosphate is presented in Figure 6 and acute pesticides intoxication is modeled in Figure 7. Pesticides absorption is often associated with inhalation or with oral route in certain cases (drinking contaminated water, etc.). The absorption function follows a decreasing exponential mathematical description since we supposed that pesticides were progressively withdrawn following intoxication. Besides this absorption function can be easily transformed into a delta Dirac function (modeling a very short term and very elevated pesticides accumulation) which has a similar mathematical description. We suppose that the absorption function was described by (15):

$$T_x(t) = P_0 e^{-\sigma * t}$$

where P_0 was fixed based on the Median Lethal Dose (LD_{50}) of values extracted from oral administration of the organophosphate Diazinon animals experiments which was reported to be around 1.250 mg/kg of body weight, meaning that from an individual of 75 kg, the LD_{50} was equal to 93 mg [62][64] and σ was arbitrarily set to 6.5 mg/h. To simplify the analysis we kept the pharmacokinetics parameters values similar to the previous case, although this might not fully depict the reality.

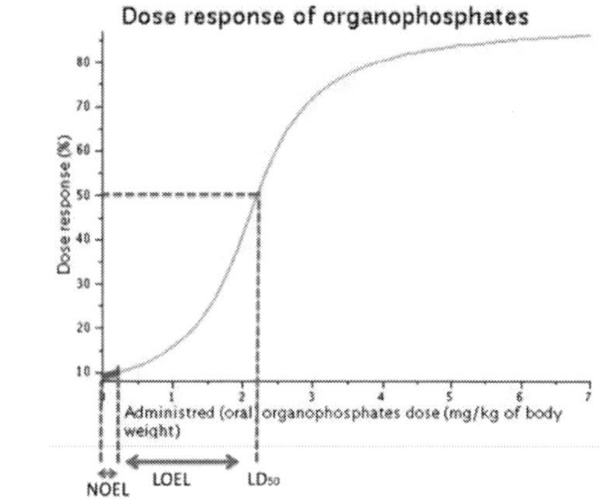

Figure 6. Dose response of specific organophosphate pesticides [62].

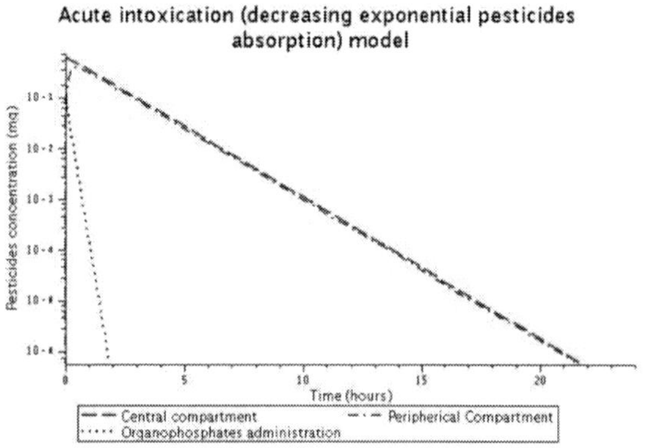

Figure 7. Acute intoxication internal body stores evolution, modeling farmer single pesticides use

5) *Mean pesticides consumption over one year:*

The pharmacokinetic model implementation results presented in Section III.2 permit to estimate the amount of organophosphates still in the CC and PC volumes with respect to time after oral dose administration each days. We wanted to further estimate the consumption of pesticides per individual over one year, based on the following assumptions:

- we supposed that for an average person, the main sources of pesticides intoxication is mainly from food and drinks consumption in accordance with [65][66].
- we estimated the pesticides ingested dose per day is between 2 and 10 mg based on National Estimate Daily Intakes (NEDIs) reports [67][70], although it may greatly vary depending on types of food consumed, quality of water drunk and general lifestyle.
- we supposed that each day, 4 meals were ingested, 3 of these with 3 between meals times of approximatively 4 hours and one between meals time of approximatively 12 hours (night).
- finally, we modeled the two different between meals times with Normal distributions of mean 4 and 12 (hours) and variance of 4 and 8 (hours) respectively.

Replacing the time by the Gaussian distribution values in the $C_c(t)$ and $C_p(t)$ functions , leads to the estimation of the amount of organophosphates stored per day in the CC and in the CP respectively.

Pesticides statistical daily accumulation in the various compartment is presented in Figure 8 and organophosphates accumulation estimation in one year in the CC and CP is illustrated in Figure 9 an may certainly explain disease rate explosion in industrialized countries.

V. CONCLUSION AND FUTURE WORK

In single organophosphates injection models (intravenous or through oral route), the concentration of pesticides in the Peripheral Compartment (PC) is greater than the concentration of pesticides in the Central Compartment (CC) in the distribution phase because the elimination of pesticides only occurs in the CC in this models. This may indicate that the blood concentration of pesticides does not accurately reflects the pesticides in other tissues, explaining why urine or hair analysis are sometimes preferred.

In the constant pesticide inhalation model, the final concentration of pesticides in the blood compartment is proportional to the amount of pesticides injected weighted by the ratio between the absorption rate (intestines, lungs, etc.) divided by the distribution and elimination parameters.

In the acute pesticides poisoning model, the CC and PC concentration of pesticides is maintained very elevated several hours after pesticides high exposure, most often requiring very quick and drastic detoxification measures.

Notwithstanding the two compartments PBPK model does describe pesticides storage in tissues only if K_d is neglected (Figure 2), which was not the case in our implementation. Including another compartment (representing pesticides long lasting body stores) or modifying our model could possibly lead to improved experimental data matching.

We estimated pesticides concentrated in blood and in other tissues, by extrapolating the organophosphates body kinetics. Since other pesticides may have very different kinetics and possibly much more elevated body accumulation, constructing PBPK models based on other pesticides types may help to better assess personal intoxication. Ultimately pesticides biomarkers studies [57] should be confronted to our model for results validation.

Pesticides blood and tissue concentration per year for an average individual is estimated to 25 mg, which however gradually grows with respect of time. Supposing that once the pesticides concentration in a certain tissue reaches a certain threshold, tissue dysfunction is expected and disease symptoms appear, such conclusions on tissue pesticides accumulation are extremely worrying and disease occurrence is unavoidable after a certain period of time. Pesticides, because of their omnipresence in foods and drinks may hence be considered as significant etiologic factors of many diseases. Consequently, measures reducing pesticides intoxication could result in a rate regression of some deceases in industrialized countries.

Backbones for user based applications of personal blood and tissue organophosphates concentration are proposed in this document and may lead to lifestyle modification.

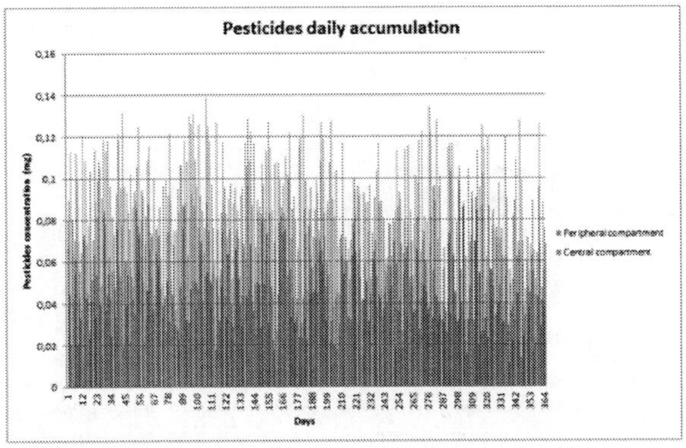

Figure 8. Pesticides daily absorption modeling of an average individual in industrialized countries

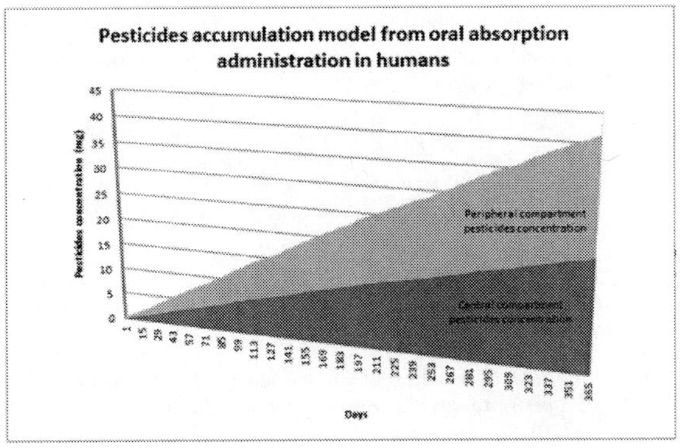

Figure 9. Pesticides accumulated in average person living in industrialized country after 1 year

REFERENCES

[1] Cdc.gov, " Pesticide Illness & Injury Surveillance - NIOSH Workplace Safety and Health Topic," 2013-09-11.

[2] G. Grullón, "Infographic: pesticide planet," *Science*, vol. 341, pp. 730-1, 2013.

[3] M. Ye, J. Beach, J. W. Martin, and A. Senthilselvan, "Occupational pesticide exposures and respiratory health," *International journal of environmental research and public health*, vol. 10, pp. 6442-6471, 2013.

[4] D. Pimentel, "Amounts of pesticides reaching target pests: environmental impacts and ethics," *Journal of Agricultural and environmental Ethics*, vol. 8, pp. 17-29, 1995.

[5] O. Zivan, M. Segal-Rosenheimer, and Y. Dubowski, "Airborne organophosphate pesticides drift in Mediterranean climate: The importance of secondary drift," *Atmospheric Environment*, vol. 127, pp. 155-162, 2016.

[6] S. Otto, D. Loddo, C. Baldoin, and G. Zanin, "Spray drift reduction techniques for vineyards in fragmented landscapes," *Journal of environmental management*, vol. 162, pp. 290-298, 2015.

[7] S. Jakuboski, "The Dangers of Pesticides," *Nature Scitable*, 201, July 25

[8] C. O. Ribeiro, Y. Vollaire, A. Sanchez-Chardi, and H. Roche, "Bioaccumulation and the effects of organochlorine pesticides, PAH and heavy metals in the Eel (Anguilla anguilla) at the Camargue Nature Reserve, France," *Aquatic Toxicology*, vol. 74, pp. 53-69, 2005.

[9] S. K. Traore *et al.*, "Contrôle des pesticides organochlorés dans le lait et produits laitiers: Bioaccumulation et risques d'exposition," *Afrique Science: Revue Internationale des Sciences et Technologie*, vol. 4, pp. 87-98, 2016.

[10] T. Katagi, "Bioconcentration, bioaccumulation, and metabolism of pesticides in aquatic organisms," in *Reviews of environmental contamination and toxicology*, ed: Springer, pp. 1-132, 2010,

[11] A. Chopra, M. K. Sharma, and S. Chamoli, "Bioaccumulation of organochlorine pesticides in aquatic system—an overview," *Environmental monitoring and assessment*, vol. 173, pp. 905-916, 2011.

[12] F. Whitford *et al.*, "The benefits of pesticides: a story worth telling," *Purdue University, Purdue Extension, West Lafayette, IN*, 2006.

[13] J. Jeyaratnam, "Acute pesticide poisoning: a major global health problem," *World Health Stat Q*, vol. 43, pp. 139-44, 1990.

[14] V. P. Androutsopoulos, A. F. Hernandez, J. Liesivuori, and A. M. Tsatsakis, "A mechanistic overview of health associated effects of low levels of organochlorine and organophosphorous pesticides," *Toxicology*, vol. 307, pp. 89-94, 2013.

[15] J. F. Shelton, I. Hertz-Picciotto, and I. N. Pessah, "Tipping the balance of autism risk: potential mechanisms linking pesticides and autism," *Environmental health perspectives*, vol. 120, p. 944, 2012.

[16] E. M. Roberts, *et al.*, "Maternal residence near agricultural pesticide applications and autism spectrum disorders among children in the California Central Valley," *Environmental health perspectives*, pp. 1482-1489, 2007.

[17] K. Lyall, R. J. Schmidt, and I. Hertz-Picciotto, "Maternal lifestyle and environmental risk factors for autism spectrum disorders," *International journal of epidemiology*, vol. 43, pp. 443-464, 2014.

[18] O. Zerbo, A.-M. Iosif, L. Delwiche, C. Walker, and I. Hertz-Picciotto, "Month of conception and risk of autism," *Epidemiology (Cambridge, Mass.)*, vol. 22, p. 469, 2011.

[19] T. B. Hayes, V. Khoury, A. Narayan, M. Nazir, A. Park, T. Brown, *et al.*, "Atrazine induces complete feminization and chemical castration in male African clawed frogs (Xenopus laevis)," *Proceedings of the National Academy of Sciences*, vol. 107, pp. 4612-4617, 2010.

[20] C. Rowe, *et al.*, "Residential proximity to organophosphate and carbamate pesticide use during pregnancy, poverty during childhood, and cognitive functioning in 10-year-old children," *Environmental Research*, vol. 150, pp. 128-137, 2016.

[21] G. D. Shapiro, *et al.*, "Exposure to organophosphorus and organochlorine pesticides, perfluoroalkyl substances, and polychlorinated biphenyls in pregnancy and the association with impaired glucose tolerance and gestational diabetes mellitus: The MIREC Study," *Environmental research*, vol. 147, pp. 71-81, 2016.

[22] S. Mostafalou and M. Abdollahi, "Pesticides and human chronic diseases: evidences, mechanisms, and perspectives," *Toxicology and applied pharmacology*, vol. 268, pp. 157-177, 2013.

[23] M. R. Bonner, *et al.*, "Occupational Exposure to Pesticides and the Incidence of Lung Cancer in the Agricultural Health Study," *Environ Health Perspect, pp. 1-31,* 2016.

[24] M. C. Alavanja, M. K. Ross, and M. R. Bonner, "Increased cancer burden among pesticide applicators and others due to pesticide exposure," *CA: A Cancer Journal for Clinicians*, vol. 63, pp. 120-142, 2013.

[25] L. C. Yee and Y. C. Wei, "Current modeling methods used in QSAR/QSPR," *Statistical Modelling of Molecular Descriptors in QSAR/QSPR, Volume 2*, pp. 1-31, 2012.

[26] C. O. X. Z.Wang, Quantitative Structure-Activity Relationship (QSAR) models", *University of Leeds*, 2013

[27] S. Lapenna, M. F. Gatnik, and A. P. Worth, *Review of QSA R Models and Software Tools for Predicting Acute and Chronic Systemic Toxicity*: Publications Office of the European Union Luxembourg, 2010.

[28] www.epa.gov., Proposed Approach to Efficiently Develop Physiologically Based Pharmacokinetic (PBPK) & Physiologically Based Pharmacokinetic-Pharmacodynamic (PBPK-PD) Models for Pesticides, [retrieved June 2016]

[29] J. B. Knaak, *et al.*, "Parameters for carbamate pesticide QSAR and PBPK/PD models for human risk assessment," in *Reviews of environmental contamination and toxicology*, ed: Springer, pp. 53-212, 2008

[30] A. J. Bednarska, P. Edwards, R. Sibly, and P. Thorbek, "A toxicokinetic model for thiamethoxam in rats: implications for higher-tier risk assessment," *Ecotoxicology*, vol. 22, pp. 548-557, 2013.

[31] S. E. Lacher, "P-Glycoprotein Transport in Pesticide Pharmacokinetics and Toxicity: Investigating a Link to Parkinson's Disease risk," 2013.

[32] S. C. Wason, T. J. Smith, M. J. Perry, and J. I. Levy, "Using physiologically-based pharmacokinetic models to incorporate chemical and non-chemical stressors into cumulative risk assessment: A case study of pesticide exposures," *International journal of environmental research and public health*, vol. 9, pp. 1971-1983, 2012.

[33] M. L. Rigas, M. S. Okino, and J. J. Quackenboss, "Use of a pharmacokinetic model to assess chlorpyrifos exposure and dose in children, based on urinary biomarker measurements," *Toxicological Sciences*, vol. 61, pp. 374-381, 2001.

[34] Z. Lin, *Integrating experimental and physiologically based pharmacokinetic modeling approaches to evaluate neurotoxicity of the herbicide atrazine across the lifespan*: uga, 2013.

[35] C. Lu, C. M. Holbrook, and L. M. Andres, "The implications of using a physiologically based pharmacokinetic (PBPK) model for pesticide risk assessment," *Environmental health perspectives*, pp. 125-130, 2010.

[36] M. Blomhøj, T. Kjeldsen, and J. Ottesen, "Compartment models," *Latest version available at: http://www4. ncsu. edu/~msolufse/Compartmentmodels. pdf*, [retrieved December 2014]

[37] R. E. Baynes, K. J. Dix, and J. E. Riviere, "Distribution and Pharmacokinetics Models," *Pesticide Biotransformation and Disposition*, p. 117, 2012.

[38] T. Joseph Kumar Reddy, and K. Pallavi. *Compartment Modelling. Vignan Pharmacy College* , 2011

[39] B. Meibohm and H. Derendorf, "Pharmacokinetic/pharmacodynamic studies in drug product development," *Journal of pharmaceutical sciences*, vol. 91, pp. 18-31, 2002.

[40] J. R. Vallabhanen. "Pharmacokinetic models", *Malla Reddy College of Pharmacy, 2014*

[41] S. R. Crowell, *et al.*, "Preliminary physiologically based pharmacokinetic models for benzo [a] pyrene and dibenzo [def, p] chrysene in rodents," *Toxicology and applied pharmacology*, vol. 257, pp. 365-376, 2011.

[42] J. C. Lipscomb, S. Haddad, T. Poet, and K. Krishnan, "Physiologically-based pharmacokinetic (PBPK) models in toxicity testing and risk assessment," in *New Technologies for Toxicity Testing*, ed: Springer, 2012, pp. 76-95.

[43] P. T. S. Office of Prevention, U.S. Environmental Protection Agency, "Physiologically-Based Pharmacokinetic/Pharmacodynamic Modeling: Preliminary Evaluation and Case Study for the N-Methyl Carbamate Pesticides," 2003.

[44] S. F. Sundlof, J. E. Riviere, and A. L. Craigmill, *Handbook of comparative veterinary pharmacokinetics and residues of pesticides and environmental contaminants*: CRC Press, 1995.

[45] R. Krieger, "Chapter 46.3 Pharmacokinetc approaches applied to organophosphae insecticides," in *Handbook of Pesticide Toxicology, Two-Volume Set: Principles and Agents*, vol. 1, ed: Academic Press, 2001.

[46] E. Hodgson, *Pesticide biotransformation and disposition*: Academic Press, 2012.

[47] S. F. Sundlof, J. E. Riviere, and A. L. Craigmill, "Principle of interspecies extrapolation," in *Handbook of comparative veterinary pharmacokinetics and residues of pesticides and environmental contaminants* ed: CRC Press, 1995, pp. 29-30.

[48] J. G. Wagner, "Properties of the Michaelis-Menten equation and its integrated form which are useful in pharmacokinetics," *Journal of pharmacokinetics and biopharmaceutics*, vol. 1, pp. 103-121, 1973.

[49] R. Mehvar, "Principles of nonlinear pharmacokinetics," *American Journal of Pharmaceutical Education*, vol. 65, p. 178, 2001.

[50] M. Stroppolo, M. Falconi, A. Caccuri, and A. Desideri, "Superefficient enzymes," *Cellular and Molecular Life Sciences CMLS*, vol. 58, pp. 1451-1460, 2001.

[51] G. Picard, and C. Trottier, (2016). *MAT-265 Équations différentielles.*

[52] M. Douai. (2016). *13. Equations differentielles lineaires du second ordre a coeficients costants*.

[53] J. Griggs. (2016). *Second-Order Linear Differential Equations*.

[54] Z. S. Tseng. (2016). *Second Order Linear Differential Equations*.

[55] M. Arrou-Vignod, and J. Millaud, (2007). *Equations differerntielles lineaires a coefficients constants, cas des equations d'ordre 1 et 2*.

[56] M.-A. Warmerdam, "Department of Pesticide Regulation," 2008.

[57] R. E. Baynes and E. Hodgson, "Absorption and distribution of toxicants," *A Textbook of Modern Toxicology*, p. 77, 2004.

[58] W. Huisinga, W. Liebermeister, and T. Jahnke, "Pharmakokinetik: Mathematische Modelle und ihre Anwendung."

[59] J. Yu, "A subcellular compartmental modeling approach to pulmonary drug development," The University of Michigan, 2011.

[60] C. Timchalk, R. Nolan, A. Mendrala, D. Dittenber, K. Brzak, and J. Mattsson, "A physiologically based pharmacokinetic and pharmacodynamic (PBPK/PD) model for the organophosphate insecticide chlorpyrifos in rats and humans," *Toxicological Sciences*, vol. 66, pp. 34-53, 2002.

[61] D. K. Singh, *Pesticide Chemistry and Toxicology*: Bentham Science Publishers, 2012.

[62] F. Whitford, T. Fuhremann, K. Rao, G. Arce, J. E. Klauning, and A. Blessing, "Pesticide toxicology: evaluationg safety and risk," in *Pesticide toxicology: evaluationg safety and risk*, ed: Pardue University, 2003.

[63] F. M. Fishel, "Pesticide Toxicity Profile: Organophosphate Pesticides," *Gainesville: University of Florida Institute of Food and Agricultural Sciences*, 2005.

[64] F. M. F. O. Norman Nesheim, and Mark Mossler. (2013). *Toxicity of Pesticides*.

[65] U. E. P. Agency. (2016). *Assessing Human Health Risk from Pesticides*.

[66] U. S. G. Survey. (2016). *Sources of nutrients and pesticides*.

[67] L. Nasreddine and D. Parent-Massin, "Food contamination by metals and pesticides in the European Union. Should we worry?," *Toxicology letters*, vol. 127, pp. 29-41, 2002.

[68] J. F. W. C. A. Commission and W. H. Organization, "Guidelines for predicting dietary intake of pesticide residues," 1997.

[69] J.-C. Leblanc, L. Malmauret, T. GuÉrin, F. Bordet, B. Boursier, and P. Verger, "Estimation of the dietary intake of pesticide residues, lead, cadmium, arsenic and radionuclides in France," *Food Additives & Contaminants*, vol. 17, pp. 925-932, 2000.

[70] S. Humbert, M. Margni, R. Charles, O. M. T. Salazar, A. L. Quirós, and O. Jolliet, "Toxicity assessment of the main pesticides used in Costa Rica," *Agriculture, ecosystems & environment*, vol. 118, pp. 183-190, 2007.

TABLE I. PHARMACOKINETIC MODEL PARAMETERS

Studied Pesticide	**PK parameters extraction**						
	Parameters	***Parameter description***	***Value***	***Species***	***Administrated Dose***	***Mode of exposure***	***References***
Thiazol-2-14C, Oxadiazin-4-14C	ka (h^{-1})	Absorption rate constant (gut)	--	Rats	0.5 mg. kg-1 body weight	intravenous exposure	{Agnieszka Bednarska(1, 2), Peter Edwards(1), Richard Sibly(3), Pernille Thorbek}
	ke (h^{-1})	Elimination rate constant (urine)	0.4				
	ka (h^{-1})	Absorption rate constant (gut)	2.2		0.5 mg. kg-1 body weight	Bolus gavage exposure	
	ke (h^{-1})	Elimination rate constant (urine)	0.25				
	ka (h^{-1})	Absorption rate constant (gut)	1.03		100 mg kg-1 body weight		
	ke (h^{-1})	Elimination rate constant (urine)	0.25				
Paraquat	CLF (L/hr)	apparent Oral Clearance	0.473	FVB Wild-type and mdr1a(-/-)/1b(-/-) Mice	--	Single Paraquat Oral Dose	[31]
	Vdss (L)	apparent Volume of Distribution	1.77				
	ka (h^{-1})	Absorption rate constant (gut)	1.81				
Atrazine	ka_{1C} (h^{-1})	Gastric absorption rate constant	0.2	Adult male C57BL/6 mice	250, 125, 25, and 5 mg/kg body weight	oral gavage for 10 days	[34]
	k_{a2C} (h^{-1})	Gastric-emptying rate constant	0.7				
	ka_{3C} (h^{-1})	Intestinal absorption rate constant	0.018				
Organophosphate Parathion and Diazinon	$t_{1/2}$ (h)	Biological half life (single compartment model)	5.08	Rabbit	1.5 mg/kg of Body Weight	Intavenous	[45]
	Vdss (l/kg)	apparent Volume of Distribution	14.24				

Studied Pesticide	PK parameters extraction						
	Parameters	***Parameter description***	***Value***	***Species***	***Administrated Dose***	***Mode of exposure***	***References***
	CL(L/h/kg)	Clearance rate	3.59				
	$t_{1/2}$ (h)	Biological half-life (single compartment model)	0.021	Rabbit	3 mg/kg of Body Weight	Oral	
	Vdss (L/kg)	apparent Volume of Distribution	7.58				
	CL(L/h/kg)	Clearance rate	--				
	$t_{1/2}^{\alpha}$ (h)	Distribution half-life (two compartments model)	0.13				
	$t_{1/2}^{\beta}$ (h)	Removal half-life (two compartments model)	1.08				
	CL(L/h/kg)	Clearance rate	6.59	Piglet	2.8 mg/kg of Body Weight	Intravenous	
	Vdss (L/kg)	Apparent volume of distribution	2.6				
	CL(L/h/kg)	Clearance rate	4.42	Pig	1 mg/kg of Body Weight	Intravenous	
	Vdss (L/kg)	Apparent volume of distribution	9.76				
	CL(L/h/kg)	Clearance rate	4.60	Rat	80 mg/kg of Body Weight	Oral	
	Vdss (L/kg)	Apparent volume of distribution	22.95				
	$t_{1/2}$ (h)	Biological half-life (single compartment model)	2.55				
	CL(L/h/kg)	Clearance rate	4.69	Rat	5 – 10 mg/kg of Body Weight	Intravenous	
	Vdss (L/kg)	Apparent volume of distribution	20.01				
	$t_{1/2}^{\alpha}$ (h)	Distribution half-life (two compartments model)	0.33				
	$t_{1/2}^{\beta}$ (h)	Elimination half-life (two compartments	4.70				

Studied Pesticide	**PK parameters extraction**						
	Parameters	***Parameter description***	***Value***	***Species***	***Administrated Dose***	***Mode of exposure***	***References***
		model only)					
TCP	k_a (h^{-1})	Absorption half-life constant	1.5	Human Volunteers	0.5 mg/kg of Body Weight		
	$t_{1/2}^{absorption}$ (h)	Absorption half-life	0.5				
	k_e (h^{-1})	Elimination rate constant	0.0258				
	$t_{1/2}^{elimination}$ (h)	Elimination half-life	20.9				
	k_a (h^{-1})	Absorption rate constant	0.0308	Human Volunteers	5 mg/ kg of Body Weight		
	$t_{1/2}^{absorption}$ (h)	Absorption half-life	22.5				
	k_e (h^{-1})	Elimination rate constant	--				
	$t_{1/2}^{absorption}$ (h)	Elimination half-life	30				

AUTHOR INDEX